SETTING UP
AND RUNNING
A LIMITED
COMPANY

SETTING UP AND RUNNING A LIMITED COMPANY

A COMPREHENSIVE GUIDE TO FORMING AND OPERATING
A COMPANY AS A DIRECTOR AND SHAREHOLDER

REVISED AND UPDATED FIFTH EDITION

ROBERT BROWNING

howtobooks

Published by How To Books Ltd
Spring Hill House, Spring Hill Road, Begbroke, Oxford OX5 1RX
Tel: (01865) 375794. Fax: (01865) 379162
info@howtobooks.co.uk
www.howtobooks.co.uk

How To Books greatly reduce the carbon footprint of their books by sourcing
their typesetting and printing in the UK.

Second edition 1999
Reprinted 1999
Third edition 2001
Fourth edition 2003
Reprinted 2004
Reprinted 2005
Reprinted 2006 (twice)
Reprinted 2007
Fifth edition 2012

British Library Cataloguing in Publication Data
A catalogue record for this book is available from the British Library

ISBN: 978 1 84528 487 9

Cover design by Baseline Arts Ltd, Oxford
Produced for How To Books by Deer Park Productions, Tavistock
Typeset by Kestrel Data, Exeter
Printed and bound in Great Britain by Bell & Bain Ltd, Glasgow

Contents

List of Illustrations

Preface
to the fifth edition

Businesses are all around you. Every time you go to the shops, the pub, the dentist or the petrol service station you are dealing with a business. While all those businesses serve you with the goods and services you want, it is normally of little consequence to you how each business is run.

Things are very different if it is your business. It is as well to know what you are getting yourself into when you start. Most lessons in life are learned the hard way. This is how you gain experience but this book is intended to help you understand the mechanics of running a business through a limited company. The aim is also to save you from as many mistakes as possible.

Remember good judgement comes from experience but experience comes from poor judgement!

You may have already started your enterprise or you may just be embarking on it but everyone can learn from others. There are many pitfalls in business life but if you can reduce or eliminate them your worries will be far less.

All businesses need a framework within which to operate but the formation of a limited company must be done for the right reasons. A lot of businesses are run through companies but there are many legal implications attached to this.

New businesses and old sometimes fail but the existence of a company will not necessarily help in those circumstances. Limited liability is not a panacea for all ills. It represents a responsibility to the general public and gives business dealings a public face. Directors, too, have onerous responsibilities.

As a chartered accountant formerly in public practice with many years' experience of small businesses, I have tried to set out simply how to decide whether establishing a company is right for you and, if so, how to go about it.

Apart from a detailed explanation of how to form and operate a company this book covers the filing of statutory information, your rights and responsibilities, the opening of bank accounts, keeping records, taxation, wages and salaries, marketing and auditing.

I would like to thank the Registrar of Companies and HMRC for the use of their forms and documentation and Messrs Baker Tilly, Chartered Accountants, for help in the original research for this book.

Any names used in the book are purely fictitious. Any similarity between the names and those of real persons is purely coincidental.

Good luck with your enterprise. As you know, your country needs you.

Robert Browning

Deciding What You Want to Do

This book is about running your business through a limited company, but first you must be clear about what you need to do. This initial chapter will help you decide this. It covers:

- starting in business

- being a sole trader or going into partnership

- buying a business

- getting professional help

- having a company or not.

STARTING IN BUSINESS

So you're going into business. You are going to become one of those entrepreneurs with a Rolls Royce and an expense account.

If only it were that easy. You have many decisions to take before you take the plunge into business.

Being in business
If you are engaged in an occupation, work or trade, whether commercial, industrial or professional, which includes the buying

and selling of services then you are in business. Note that there is no mention of the word **profit**. Of course, you would not be in business if you were not going to make a profit but it is not compulsory, just advisable.

This book is not intended to help you set up a business. It assumes you already have a product or service that you wish to sell or trade in. This book is designed to help you administer the business you have set up.

Owning your business

Asking who owns your business may seem a silly question but there can easily be other people involved. Your spouse or partner or son or daughter may work in the business or someone may have lent you some money to start it up. You must make sure that you know precisely the relationship any of these people have with you in your enterprise so that their interest can be properly taken into account.

Problems in business invariably arise through sloppy arrangements about money, so be advised to clarify these at the start.

Naming your business

There are a number of factors to take into account when deciding what to call your business. These are more fully discussed in Chapter 7, but you must choose a suitable name as this is what the public will refer to when talking about your business.

Defining your business

It is as well to define precisely what product or service your business is going to supply. Not only must you be able to inform your potential customers what you do but you must also be able to market and advertise your wares simply but succinctly. You must make it easy for your customer to deal with you.

BEING A SOLE TRADER OR GOING INTO PARTNERSHIP

Creating your set-up

You have established that you have a business with a name and a product or service to sell. You know who the owner is. You must now consider the implications of this. You have to decide what legal form your business will take. You can be a:

■ sole trader

■ partnership.

Being a sole trader

The word 'sole' in this context means alone or the one and only. In business terms a **sole trader** is where the proprietor is the sole owner of a business although he or she may have employees.

Being a partnership

A **partnership** is defined by law in the Partnership Act 1890. It is the relationship which subsists between persons carrying on a business in common with a view to profit.

Put another way it is the relationship between people who have agreed to share the profits of a business carried on by all or any of them on behalf of all of them.

It might be advantageous to examine a little history. In the Middle Ages, when trading was growing fast, individual traders found considerable advantage in combining with each other to carry on their business. The advantage was that it enabled them to command greater amounts of **capital** money they could not individually bring together and it helped them to combine and share their common experience and their profits. This was the beginning of partnerships.

Now if you have an arrangement to share the profits of your business with another person, the chances are that you are in partnership, sometimes known as a **firm**. This may be a close friend with whom you have a rapport and would work well or someone who may have put money into your business. There is now, under the Limited Liability Partnerships Act 2000, the opportunity to form a partnership with **limited liability**. It must be registered with the Registrar of Companies and two of the partners, called 'designated members', must accept responsibility for sending information to Companies House. This form of partnership is treated for tax purposes like any other.

BUYING A BUSINESS

While thinking of going into business it may have occurred to you that it might be simpler to buy a ready-made business. After all, the hard slog of building up your customer base would be eliminated. The premises would already exist. There may be some staff and the stock may already be in the warehouse.

Don't be misled.

Why is the owner selling? Have you the money to compensate the owner for building it up? Suppose you pay too much. If you are thinking of buying a business to make life easy, think again. Being in business is about responsibility.

There is no easy way to establishing your own business.

Seven steps to making your decision

Here is a simple guide to what you should consider when buying a business.

1. If you are already in business what are you looking to add?
    - Have you money to invest?
    - Have you expertise that can be employed in the additional business?

2. Define the business profile you would like to acquire.
    - Why will you be successful?
    - What size business are you looking for?
    - Where should it be located?

3. Learn about your market and do the research.
    - What are the growth areas?
    - What are the products you expect to sell?

4. What are the sources of businesses for sale?
    - Where will you find businesses advertised for sale?
    - What are the newspapers, magazines, business transfer agents and trade organisations which can help?

- Sift through them carefully and investigate the ones that match your profile.
- Consider suitable businesses which fit your profile but where the owner may not have decided to sell.

5. What effect will you have on the business if you buy it?
    - Will you be able to run it?
    - Have you the necessary knowledge of the business or the management skills?
    - Will you increase the profitability?
    - What changes will you make?

6. What is the maximum price you are prepared to pay?
    - Have you got up-to-date copies of the accounts of the business?
    - What are the profits?
    - How much money is invested in the business and is the return on capital good enough?
    - What are the **debts** and **liabilities** and have any been outstanding for a long time?

7. Are you ready to negotiate?
    - Have you got your facts prepared?
    - Are you ready to make a decision?

These questions are by no means exhaustive but they give you an idea of the things you should be considering before you put your money into a new venture.

Summary

1. Don't be tempted to pay too much for the business because you think it will give you a flying start.

2. Make sure you are entering a marketplace you can compete in.

3. Clarify the business you want to be in including its size, location and potential.

4. Be realistic about the effect of a change of ownership.

5. Question everything.

6. Crystallise your negotiating position. Know your top price and the one you are prepared to start at and stick to them. There is no such thing as a right price.

7. Obtain all the help you can from independent professional advisers (accountants, bankers, solicitors, surveyors, etc.).

GETTING PROFESSIONAL HELP

Too many people either think they know it all or trust to luck when it comes to business matters. But even the most successful entrepreneur will tell you that they are always ready to listen to sound advice. The problem is how to know it is sound. That comes with experience.

It is best to seek out the right professional advisers as early in your planning as possible. They may come up with advice which can materially affect the way your business operates and you can incorporate it before the process gets too far. It is important to avoid errors and misjudgements before they happen, and unless this is done you may start your business with a permanent handicap.

Business advice can be obtained from:

■ accountants

■ bankers

■ financial planners

■ solicitors

■ surveyors and estate agents.

Here are some points to watch.

Accountants

The term **'accountants'** does not necessarily mean they have any formal qualification. But you would be well advised to find an accountant who is a member of a recognised association as you will have some guarantee that he or she has followed a course of training and passed examinations in the skills required. The main bodies are:

■ the Institute of Chartered Accountants in England & Wales (with FCA or ACA after their name)

■ the Institute of Chartered Accountants of Scotland (CA)

■ the Chartered Association of Certified Accountants (FCCA or ACCA)

■ the Institute of Management Consultants (FIMA or AIMA), who deal mainly in management consultancy work as their name implies.

The cost should be discussed and agreed before any work is carried out.

Bankers

Banks offer a wide range of services including current accounts, loans and assistance with imports and exports. A particular bank can be chosen for a number of reasons, for example convenience, knowledge of the staff or even to separate your business accounts from your personal affairs. Larger branches have more discretionary powers as they do not have to pass decisions up to regional managers for approval but these would only be used when substantial funds are required.

Shop around to find out what it will cost to run your account.

Financial planners

They may help you in your marketing strategy, your budget projections, your organisation or the amount of money you may need to get your business off the ground. It is difficult to choose one but most large accountancy practices have specialist sections. You will normally be charged a flat fee based on your requirements.

Solicitors

A **solicitor** will be particularly useful in advising on the legal form of your business, the formation of your company, any contracts you may enter into and registration of patents and product protection. Costs vary but a solicitor will normally give you an estimate and some may give you a package deal. Fees must be 'fair and reasonable' by law.

Solicitors also specialise so make sure you get one who can deal with your needs. The larger the firm the bigger the range of activities they are likely to cover.

Surveyors and estate agents

Any transactions involving land or buildings will need the expertise of a **surveyor** to assure you that you are not entering into a contract unwisely. Matters covered include:

■ surveys of premises

■ planning permissions or change of the use of premises

■ rates and rateable values

■ whether the title is leasehold or freehold

■ repairs and maintenance clauses in agreements.

The recognised body is the Royal Institution of Chartered Surveyors (FRICS or ARICS). If you are involved in the valuations you could use the services of a member of the Incorporated Society of Valuers and Auctioneers.

Costs are again a matter of negotiation and agreement.

With all the above professional advisers do not hesitate to take out references or seek advice from people you know who use them. Personal recommendations from friends and colleagues are usually sound.

HAVING A COMPANY OR NOT

You now have to decide whether you want to trade through a company or not. Like life itself there are advantages and disadvantages in everything but the decision has to be taken. Nothing is irrevocable but remember there is always a cost. It is far better to weigh up the pros and cons first.

How the company was born

Look at a little history again.

When trade increased dramatically in the 19th century traders began to get together and run their businesses jointly. However, the increased activity also increased the burdens on individual partners. The property and debts of the firm were considered to be the property and debts of the individual partners. Therefore partnerships had no legal existence apart from the individual partners.

Then in 1844 an Act of Parliament was passed for the Registration of Joint Stock Companies. Such an incorporated company could now hold property, incur debts and sue and be sued in its own name. The members (or partners) were no longer responsible for such matters individually. This was known as limited liability.

Differences between a company and a partnership or sole trader

Some of the differences are:

	Partnership or sole trader	Company
Members' liability	Unlimited	Limited
Number of members	Limited	Unlimited
Transfer of interest	Only with consent of other partners	Shares may be transferred
Capital introduced	By arrangement with other partners	Fixed by company rules
Profit sharing	-ditto-	-ditto-

Advantages of a company and of a partnership

Advantages of a company

1. A **company** has limited liability and it does not extend to the separate assets of each member whereas a partner's liabilities are not limited and extend, if necessary, to the whole of their individual estates.

2. The shares of a company are easily transferred but the value of the interest of a partner is much more difficult to determine.

3. The death of a company member does not affect the existence of a company. If a partner dies, however, the partnership ceases to exist.

4. Profits of a company are distributed by way of dividends which are unearned for tax purposes whereas profits of a partnership are earned income. However, the tax changes

which continually take place with the Budget and subsequent **Finance Acts** can drastically alter how each of these is treated and should be checked at the time.

Advantages of a partnership

1. A partnership may tend to give a more personal aspect to dealings.

2. There are no heavy setting-up expenses to a partnership.

3. The activities of the partnership are not subject to restriction as with a company, which is limited by the **Objects clause** in its **Memorandum of Association**. Currently Objects clauses allow almost anything that is legal.

4. Partners may override the Partnership Act by agreement amongst themselves whereas companies have to abide by the Companies Acts.

5. All partners can take part in the management of the business and no change in the constitution can take place without the consent of all the partners. In a company the will of the majority operates but the company is normally run day to day by the board of directors.

6. Partnerships have no registration formalities.

You should by now have considered all aspects of your business and have made up your mind whether you would like to run your business through a company. The rest of this book explains in detail how to go about it.

ACTION POINTS AND REMINDERS

1. Who are the people directly involved in your business and what do they contribute to it?

2. Consider all the possible names you might wish to call your business.

3. Are you sure of all the products or services you intend to supply from your business?

4. Will you be a sole trader or do you need a partner?

5. Are you contemplating purchasing a ready-made business? If so, where from?

6. Name, if applicable, your possible accountant, banker, financial planner, solicitor and surveyor.

If, as a result of completing these answers, you are convinced that you wish to form a company proceed to Chapter 2.

Setting up and Forming Your Company

Now that you have made up your mind to run your business through a company, this chapter tells you what to think about and how to plan it and includes:

■ creating a separate entity

■ defining your objects

■ calculating your capital

■ issuing shares

■ acquiring your company.

CREATING A SEPARATE ENTITY

This is fundamental.

What is a company?

In Chapter 1 you read how the concept of partnership came about and how as trade increased there was more and more of a burden on the individual partners. The property and the debts of the firm were considered to be the property and debts of the individual partners. In the nature of things partners died and, as they were no longer partners, the partnership ceased to exist.

By the mid 19th century a more permanent form of partnership evolved, known as the **joint stock company**.

This meant that a company could hold property, incur debts and sue and be sued in its own name. This was known as 'limited liability' and meant that the members (partners) were no longer personally liable for the debts of the company.

As a result of this the company exists permanently and is in effect an 'artificial' person, quite separate from the individual members of the company.

This is an important principle to be grasped:
In your business dealings
it is not *you* that is dealing
but *you on behalf of your company*.

From now on whenever the word 'company' is used please remember this important principle. All detailed legislation relating to limited companies is contained in the **Companies Act** 2006. This is now the main statutory act for UK company law.

Preparing for your application

Your first job is to complete form IN01: Application to register a company. This is a comprehensive form designed to give the **Registrar of Companies** full details of your proposed company (see Chapter 4).

You must therefore make sure you have made decisions about your company name and cleared it with the Registrar of Companies. You must also decide where your address will be so that anyone can get in touch with you, and where certain statutory information will be held.

Choosing the name

You can choose any name you wish, subject to a few obvious conditions. You may not choose a name if:

(a) it is already registered by someone else

(b) it requires the approval of the Secretary of State because it is 'sensitive'; this could be so if, for example, it contains the words, International, British, European, etc.

(c) it contains words which other relevant bodies might object to: for example, Police, Royal, Charity, etc

This list is by no means exhaustive but you can see the difficulties that may arise if your intended name is too similar to that of another company or gives the impression that it is something which it is not. Watch this carefully as another company could object and your company be directed to change its name with the additional expense that entails.

> **Be careful to clear your intended name with the Registrar of Companies first.**

Example

Acceptable   –   Chapman Security Ltd.

Not acceptable   –   Police Security Systems Ltd.

DEFINING YOUR OBJECTS

There is no requirement, either in the Memorandum or Articles of Association, for companies to state their objects.

Although a company can, as a separate legal entity, acquire rights and incur liabilities, its powers are slightly less extensive than a real person. A real person can do anything not prohibited by law but a company is restricted to a classification that defines the type of economic activity in which it is engaged. It is not necessary to go into great detail here as the main object of the business will be defined by a classification that will not inhibit the company from carrying out any object it wishes.

In other words, for all intents and purposes, you will be able to do anything within reason and within the law.

CALCULATING YOUR CAPITAL

Your capital requirements will depend on the type of business you are contemplating, but your **share capital** must be defined as a number of **shares** with a nominal value.

For example: The share capital of the company is divided into 1,000 ordinary shares of £1 each.

There can be different classes of shares but for this purpose we will assume there is only one.

You will also have to name the subscribers for those shares and how many each will take. If you wish to take complete control of your company you must subscribe for at least 50 per cent of the shares yourself.

A share limits the liability of the **shareholder**. In simple terms it means that no **member**, meaning a shareholder, is liable to contribute any more than the value of his shares. Once you have paid for your shares that is the extent of your liability. This is obviously a comforting thought if anything goes wrong.

Example

Your authorised capital is 1,000 ordinary shares of £1 each. Two are normally issued to start with and these are transferred from the agent to yourself and your other shareholder. (It is possible, but not unusual, for a company to be formed with only one shareholder.) This leaves a further 998 shares to be issued. You may decide to issue 498 of those, split between yourself and the other shareholder so that you finish up with 400 and he holds 100. This is known as **issued** or **paid up** capital. This gives you control of the company (more fully described in Chapter 5).

	You	*Other*
Subscriber shares	1	1
Allotment	399	99
Final shareholding	400	100
Authorised capital still to be issued	500 shares	

Note that the authorised capital of a company can only be changed or increased in accordance with the Articles of the company (see Chapter 3, p. 55).

ISSUING SHARES

The concept of issuing shares is simple. Shares have a nominal value of, say, £1 each and when they are issued to a prospective shareholder he pays £1 for them. That is the limit of his liability towards the debts and obligations of the company.

Example

1. You buy 500 shares of £1 each for £500 and the money goes into the company's bank account as part of its assets.

2. You will not have to buy any more if you do not wish but the implications of doing so are discussed in Chapter 9.

3. This capital will remain fixed within the company and will be repayable to you as a shareholder only when the company is closed down (when you will receive, for each of your shares, the value of the company's assets divided by the number of shares issued) or in certain circumstances when the company wishes to buy back the shares from you.

4. You are, of course, at liberty to sell the shares to another person and this can be at any price you negotiate between you and not necessarily at the £1 you originally purchased them for.

The Memorandum of Association of a company having a share capital will now be required to submit a form showing the subscribers of shares (see Figure 1).

COMPANY HAVING A SHARE CAPITAL

Memorandum of association of Sinclair Brook Ltd

Each subscriber to this memorandum of association wishes to form a company under the Companies Act 2006 and agrees to become a member of the company and to take at least one share.

Name of each subscriber	Authentication by each subscriber
Simon Browning	
Matthew Browning	
Leesa Browning	

Dated   15 November 20XX

Fig. 1. Memorandum for a company having a share capital (CA2006).

ACQUIRING YOUR COMPANY

There are two ways of setting yourself up in business. You can do this by:

■ starting a business on your own or in partnership

■ buying an existing business.

Either of these can be put into a company and, indeed, the latter may already exist as a company.

Starting your own business

If you are setting up your business on your own you may wish to start with a brand new company. This can be done in two ways.

1. Buy a new or custom-made company with your own choice of name. Various forms will have to be signed.

2. Buy a ready-made company which has never traded. This is known as buying a company **off the shelf**.

Both of these methods can most easily be done through a **company formation** or **registration agent**. A telephone call to one of them will set the ball rolling but you must have your company name and address ready. Alternatively, the agent will have a bank of ready-made companies already named for you to choose from if you wish.

The agent will then send you the details of the company with your chosen name. They will also probably arrange for the original subscriber shares to be issued. A company may exist with only one shareholder but there will normally be more. The shares are normally put in the agent's and a colleague's name for convenience as it saves having to get your signature every time something needs to be done.

What about the cost?

You will at this stage have to pay an amount of say £100 depending on the amount contained in the agent's package. This may be an economy package containing the basic legal requirements with a simple register of the company's history. It may be a regular package with additional copies of your Memorandum and Articles and a better register, or it may be a deluxe package with a brass name plate and your **Certificate of Incorporation** in a frame. It will be your choice but you should have more, rather than fewer, copies of the Memorandum and Articles as these may be useful when dealing with banks and other funders who may wish to see or retain a copy.

Once all the forms have been signed and sent to the Registrar of Companies and you have received your Certificate of Incorporation (see Figure 2) you are ready to trade.

Buying an existing business

The purchase of an existing company has many facets to be considered:

■ What are you buying?

■ Is it what you want?

■ Do you only want the assets of the business?

CERTIFICATE OF INCORPORATION

OF A PRIVATE LIMITED COMPANY

Company No. 2958141

The Registrar of Companies for England and Wales hereby certifies that
SINCLAIR BROOK LIMITED

is this day incorporated under the Companies Act 1985 as a private

company and that the company is limited.

Given at Companies House, Cardiff, the 12th August XXXX

For the Registrar of Companies

C O M P A N I E S   H O U S E

HC007A

Fig. 2. Certificate of Incorporation.

■ Is there any goodwill?

■ How much are the shares?

Remember the company is a legal entity on its own so when you buy it you buy all its debts and liabilities as well as its assets. Now note the legal requirements of purchasing an existing company.

If you buy an existing business which is in a company you will not have to go through as much formality. The company is already in existence with an acceptable name. All you have to do from a legal viewpoint, therefore, is to transfer the shares into the names of your intended shareholders and submit to the Registrar of Companies the changes in directors, secretary and registered office.

You are now ready to commence trading with your newly acquired company.

> **Be careful how you issue your shares.**

Control

The control of the company, which is the power to decide who are the directors and what the business does, rests with the shareholders. Each share they hold gives them a vote or say in the affairs of the company and therefore the more you hold the greater the say. It follows that if you hold more than half the shares you will have more than half the say and 51 per cent of the shares in a company gives you effective control of it.

In practice the shareholders normally elect the directors and it is they who decide on the day-to-day running of the company. Only in exceptional circumstances will the shareholders exercise their right to overturn a decision of the directors. There are some decisions that require 75 per cent of the voting members, but these are rare and fundamental to the organisation of the company.

It is therefore important to issue your shares with these thoughts in mind. If you want complete control of your company you must have more than 75 per cent of the shares.

The issue of shares in a new company is done by means of an **allotment** of the shares to the first shareholders. Form SH01, which shows how they have been allotted, must be submitted to the Registrar of Companies (see Figure 3). This shows the total number of shares allotted and the names and addresses of the shareholders and must be signed and submitted by a director or the secretary within 21 days of the allotment. There is no limit to the number of shareholders except that there cannot be more than the number of shares in issue. However, joint shareholders are permitted.

The receipt of the shareholder's money is acknowledged by the preparation of a **share certificate** (see Figure 4). This gives ownership or title to the shares, and must be passed back to the company for re-issue if the shares change hands.

When shares change hands it is done by means of a **stock transfer form** (see Figure 5) which is lodged with the **company secretary**, who will then issue the certificate to the new shareholder.

SH01
Return of allotment of shares

Companies House
for the record

You can use the WebFiling service to file this form online.
Please go to www.companieshouse.gov.uk

✓ **What this form is for**
You may use this form to give
notice of shares allotted following
incorporation.

✗ **What this form is NOT for**
You cannot use this form to give
notice of shares taken by subscribers
on formation of the company or
for an allotment of a new class of
shares by an unlimited company.

For further information, please
refer to our guidance at
www.companieshouse.gov.uk

---

1   **Company details**

Company number	2 9 5 8 1 4 1
Company name in full	SINCLAIR BROOK LTD

→ **Filling in this form**
Please complete in typescript or in
bold black capitals.

All fields are mandatory unless
specified or indicated by *

---

2   **Allotment dates** ❶

From Date	ᵈ1 ᵈ5	ᵐ1 ᵐ1	ʸ2 ʸ0 ʸX ʸX
To Date	ᵈ ᵈ	ᵐ ᵐ	ʸ ʸ ʸ ʸ

❶ **Allotment date**
If all shares were allotted on the
same day enter that date in the
'from date' box. If shares were
allotted over a period of time,
complete both 'from date' and 'to
date' boxes.

---

3   **Shares allotted**

Please give details of the shares allotted, including bonus shares.
(Please use a continuation page if necessary.)

❷ **Currency**
If currency details are not
completed we will assume currency
is in pound sterling.

Class of shares (E.g. Ordinary/Preference etc.)	Currency ❷	Number of shares allotted	Nominal value of each share	Amount paid (including share premium) on each share	Amount (if any) unpaid (including share premium) on each share
ORDINARY		1000	£1	£1	

If the allotted shares are fully or partly paid up otherwise than in cash, please
state the consideration for which the shares were allotted.

Continuation page
Please use a continuation page if
necessary.

Details of non-cash
consideration.

If a PLC, please attach
valuation report (if
appropriate)

CHFP000
03/11 Version 5.0

Fig. 3. Return of allotment of shares (Form SH01).

SH01
Return of allotment of shares

Statement of capital

Section 4 (also Section 5 and Section 6, if appropriate) should reflect the company's issued capital at the date of this return.

4   **Statement of capital** (Share capital in pound sterling (£))

Please complete the table below to show each class of shares held in pound sterling. If all your issued capital is in sterling, only complete Section 4 and then go to Section 7.

Class of shares (E.g. Ordinary/Preference etc.)	Amount paid up on each share ❶	Amount (if any) unpaid on each share ❶	Number of shares ❷	Aggregate nominal value ❸
ORDINARY	£1		£1000	£ 1000
				£
				£
				£
			Totals	£

5   **Statement of capital** (Share capital in other currencies)

Please complete the table below to show any class of shares held in other currencies.
Please complete a separate table for each currency.

Currency

Class of shares (E.g. Ordinary / Preference etc.)	Amount paid up on each share ❶	Amount (if any) unpaid on each share ❶	Number of shares ❷	Aggregate nominal value ❸
			Totals	

Currency

Class of shares (E.g. Ordinary/Preference etc.)	Amount paid up on each share ❶	Amount (if any) unpaid on each share ❶	Number of shares ❷	Aggregate nominal value ❸
			Totals	

6   **Statement of capital** (Totals)

Please give the total number of shares and total aggregate nominal value of issued share capital.

❸ Total aggregate nominal value
Please list total aggregate values in different currencies separately. For example: £100 + €100 + $10 etc.

Total number of shares	1000
Total aggregate nominal value ❸	£1000

❶ Including both the nominal value and any share premium.
❷ Total number of issued shares in this class.
❸ E.g. Number of shares issued multiplied by nominal value of each share.

Continuation Pages
Please use a Statement of Capital continuation page if necessary.

CHFP000
03/11 Version 5.0

Fig. 3. (continued).

SH01
Return of allotment of shares

7 | Statement of capital (Prescribed particulars of rights attached to shares)

Please give the prescribed particulars of rights attached to shares for each class of share shown in the statement of capital share tables in **Section 4** and **Section 5**.

Class of share

Prescribed particulars ❶

Class of share

Prescribed particulars ❶

Class of share

Prescribed particulars ❶

❶ Prescribed particulars of rights attached to shares

The particulars are:
a particulars of any voting rights, including rights that arise only in certain circumstances;
b particulars of any rights, as respects dividends, to participate in a distribution;
c particulars of any rights, as respects capital, to participate in a distribution (including on winding up); and
d whether the shares are to be redeemed or are liable to be redeemed at the option of the company or the shareholder and any terms or conditions relating to redemption of these shares.

A separate table must be used for each class of share.

Continuation page
Please use a Statement of Capital continuation page if necessary.

8 | Signature

I am signing this form on behalf of the company.

Signature

Signature

X   X

This form may be signed by:
Director ❷, Secretary, Person authorised ❸, Administrator, Administrative receiver, Receiver, Receiver manager, CIC manager.

❷ Societas Europaea
If the form is being filed on behalf of a Societas Europaea (SE) please delete 'director' and insert details of which organ of the SE the person signing has membership.

❸ Person authorised
Under either section 270 or 274 of the Companies Act 2006.

CHFP000
03/11 Version 5.0

Fig. 3. (continued).

SH01
Return of allotment of shares

👤 Presenter information

You do not have to give any contact information, but if you do it will help Companies House if there is a query on the form. The contact information you give will be visible to searchers of the public record.

Contact name

Company name

Address

Post town

County/Region

Postcode

Country

DX

Telephone

✓ Checklist

We may return the forms completed incorrectly or with information missing.

Please make sure you have remembered the following:
- ☐ The company name and number match the information held on the public Register.
- ☐ You have shown the date(s) of allotment in section 2.
- ☐ You have completed all appropriate share details in section 3.
- ☐ You have completed the appropriate sections of the Statement of Capital.
- ☐ You have signed the form.

❗ Important information

Please note that all information on this form will appear on the public record.

✉ Where to send

You may return this form to any Companies House address, however for expediency we advise you to return it to the appropriate address below:

For companies registered in England and Wales:
The Registrar of Companies, Companies House,
Crown Way, Cardiff, Wales, CF14 3UZ.
DX 33050 Cardiff.

For companies registered in Scotland:
The Registrar of Companies, Companies House,
Fourth floor, Edinburgh Quay 2,
139 Fountainbridge, Edinburgh, Scotland, EH3 9FF.
DX ED235 Edinburgh 1
or LP - 4 Edinburgh 2 (Legal Post).

For companies registered in Northern Ireland:
The Registrar of Companies, Companies House,
Second Floor, The Linenhall, 32-38 Linenhall Street,
Belfast, Northern Ireland, BT2 8BG.
DX 481 N.R. Belfast 1.

ℹ Further information

For further information please see the guidance notes on the website at www.companieshouse.gov.uk or email enquiries@companieshouse.gov.uk

This form is available in an alternative format. Please visit the forms page on the website at www.companieshouse.gov.uk

This form has been provided free of charge by Companies House.

CHFP000
03/11 Version 5.0

Fig. 3. (continued).

SHARE CERTIFICATE

Certificate No.......1.............

Date.......15ᵀᴴ AUGUST 200X

No. of Shares.......1 To 500

SINCLAIR BROOK LIMITED

(Registered in England No. 2958141)

THIS IS TO CERTIFY that the undermentioned is/are the registered holder(s) of
fully paid Ordinary Shares of £1 each in Sinclair Brook Limited
subject to the Memorandum and Articles of Association of the Company.

NAME(S) OF HOLDER(S)

NUMBER OF SHARES

Mathew Alexander Browning

500 (FIVE HUNDRED)

27 Haileybury Street
Melbourne
Herts.
SG 27 8KK

GIVEN under the Seal of the Company

Note: No transfer of any portion of this holding will be registered unless this certificate is deposited at the Registered Office of the Company.

THIS DOCUMENT IS VALUABLE AND SHOULD BE KEPT IN A SAFE PLACE.

Fig. 4. Share certificate.

STOCK TRANSFER FORM

The LONDON LAW AGENCY LIMITED

Company Registration agents

Law Agents

Printers and Publishers

Temple Chambers Temple Avenue London EC4Y 0HP 0171-353 9471)

(Above this line for Registrars only)

Certificate lodged with the Registrar

Consideration Money £ **50**

(For completion by the Registrar/Stock Exchange)

Name of Undertaking **SINCLAIR BROOK LIMITED**

Description of Security **ORDINARY SHARES OF £1 EACH**

Number or amount of Shares, Stock or other security and, in figures columns only, number and denomination of units, if any

Words

FIFTY ORDINARY SHARES OF £1 EACH

Figures

50

(**50** units of **£1**)

Name(s) of registered holder(s) should be given in full; the address should be given where there is only one holder.

If the transfer is not made by the registered holder(s) insert also the name(s) and capacity (e.g. Executor(s)) of the person(s) making the transfer

In the name(s) of

MATHEW ALEXANDER BROWNING
27 HAILEYBURY STREET,
MELBOURNE,
HERTS. SG27 8KK

I/We hereby transfer the above security out of the name(s) aforesaid to the person(s) named below or to the several persons named in Parts 2 of Brokers Transfer Forms relating to the above security.

Delete words in italics except for stock exchange transactions

Signature(s) of transferor(s)

1. **MA Browning**

2. ....

3. ....

4. ....

Bodies corporate should execute under their common seal.

Stamp of Selling Broker(s) or, for transactions which are not stock exchange transactions, of Agent(s), if any, acting for the Transferor(s).

Date

Full name(s) and full postal address(es) (including County or, if applicable, Postal District number) of the person(s) to whom the security is transferred.

Please state title, if any, or whether Mr., Mrs. or Miss.

Please complete in typewriting or in Block Capitals.

SIMON BROWNING
62 FARMERS ROAD
BRAUGHING,
HERTS. SG17 7AX

I/We request that such entries be made in the register as are necessary to give effect to this transfer.

Stamp of Buying Broker(s) (if any)

Stamp or name and address of person lodging this form (if other than the Buying Broker(s))

Fig. 5. Stock transfer form.

FORM OF CERTIFICATE REQUIRED WHERE TRANSFER IS EXEMPT FROM STAMP DUTY

Instruments executed on or after 1st May 1987 effecting any transactions within the following categories are exempt from stamp duty:—

A. The vesting of property subject to a trust in the trustees of the trust on the appointment of a new trustee, or in the continuing trustees on the retirement of a trustee.

B. The conveyance or transfer of property the subject of a specific devise or legacy to the beneficiary named in the will (or his nominee). Transfers in satisfaction of a general legacy of money should not be included in this category (see category D below).

C. The conveyance or transfer of property which forms part of an intestate's estate to the person entitled on intestacy (or his nominee). Transfers in satisfaction of the transferees entitlement to cash in the estate of an intestate, where the total value of the residuary estate exceeds that sum, should not be included in this category (see category D below).

D. The appropriation of property within section 84(4) of the Finance Act 1985 (death: appropriation in satisfaction of a general legacy of money) or section 84(5) or (7) of that Act (death: appropriation in satisfaction of any interest of surviving spouse and in Scotland also of any interest of issue).

E. The conveyance or transfer of property which forms part of the residuary estate of a testator to a beneficiary (or his nominee) entitled solely by virtue of his entitlement under the will.

F. The conveyance or transfer of property out of a settlement in or towards satisfaction of a beneficiary's interest, not being an interest acquired for money or money's worth, being a conveyance or transfer constituting a distribution of property in accordance with the provisions of the settlement.

G. The conveyance or transfer of property on and in consideration only of marriage to a party to the marriage (or his nominee) or to trustees to be held on the terms of a settlement made in consideration only of the marriage. A transfer to a spouse after the date of marriage is not within this category, unless made pursuant to an ante-nuptial contract.

H. The conveyance or transfer of property within section 83(1) of the Finance Act 1985 (transfers in connection with divorce etc.).

I. The conveyance or transfer by the liquidator of property which formed part of the assets of the company in liquidation to a shareholder of that company (or his nominee) in or towards satisfaction of the shareholder's rights on a winding-up.

J. The grant in fee simple of an easement in or over land for no consideration in money or money's worth.

K. The grant of a servitude for no consideration in money or money's worth.

L. The conveyance or transfer of property operating as a voluntary disposition inter vivos for no consideration in money or money's worth nor any consideration referred to in section 57 of the Stamp Act 1891 (conveyance in consideration of a debt etc.).

M. The conveyance or transfer of property by an instrument within section 84(1) of the Finance Act 1985 (death: varying disposition).

(1) Delete as appropriate (2) Insert "(A)", "(B)" or appropriate category. (3) Delete second sentence if the certificate is given by the transferor or his solicitor	(1) I/We hereby certify that the transaction in respect of which this transfer is made is one which falls within the category(2) above. (1)I/We confirm that (1)I/We have been duly authorised by the transferor to sign this certificate and that the facts of the transaction are within (1)my/our knowledge (3)

Signature(s)   Description ("Transferor", "Solicitor", etc.)

....

....

....

Date .... 19......

NOTES
(1) If the above certificate has been completed, this transfer does not need to be submitted to the Controller of Stamps but should be sent directly to the Company or its Registrars.
(2) If the above certificate is not completed, this transfer must be submitted to the Controller of Stamps and duly stamped. (See below).

FORM OF CERTIFICATE REQUIRED WHERE TRANSFER IS NOT EXEMPT BUT IS NOT LIABLE TO AD VALOREM STAMP DUTY

Instruments of transfer, other than those in respect of which the above certificate has been completed, are liable to a fixed duty of 50p when the transaction falls within one of the following categories:—

(a) Transfer by way of security for a loan or re-transfer to the original transferor on repayment of a loan.

(b) Transfer, not on sale and not arising under any contract of sale and where no beneficial interest in the property passes: (i) to a person who a mere nominee of, and is nominated only by, the transferor; (ii) from a mere nominee who has at all times held the property on behalf of transferee; (iii) from one nominee to another nominee of the same beneficial owner where the first nominee has at all times held the property on behalf of that beneficial owner. (NOTE—This category does not include a transfer made in any of the following circumstances: (i) by a holder of stock, etc., following the grant of an option to purchase the stock, to the person entitled to the option or his nominee; (ii) to a person in contemplation of a contract for the sale of the stock, etc., then about to be entered into; (iii) from the nominee of a vendor, who has instructed the nominee orally or by some unstamped writing to hold stock, etc., in trust for a purchaser, to such purchaser.)

(1) Delete as appropriate. (2) Insert "(a)", "(b)". (3) Here set out concisely the facts explaining the transaction. Adjudication may be required.	(1) I/We hereby certify that the transaction in respect of which this transfer is made is one which falls within the category(2) above. (1)I/we confirm that (1)I/We have been duly authorised by the transferor to sign this certificate and that the facts of the transaction are within (1)my/our knowledge. (3)...

....

....

....

....

Signature(s)   Description ("Transferor", "Solicitor", etc.)

....

....

....

Date........................... 19......

Fig. 5. (continued).

Action Points and Reminders

1. List three possible names you could choose for your company.

2. Decide who you will ask to be shareholders.

3. Consider who you would choose as co-directors.

4. Decide who you would like to be company secretary bearing in mind the legal obligations of that office. You may like to do it yourself.

5. Decide how much capital the company will need.

6. Decide how many shares you intend to hold yourself.

7. You must now find a company agent who can help you form your company.

Dealing with the Formalities

Like many things in life there is a certain amount of bureaucracy to be dealt with in starting a company. This chapter looks at some of the procedures to be gone through in order to get your company up and running. They include:

- understanding the company's Articles of Association

- appointing your directors and secretary

- getting a registered office

- displaying your certificate of incorporation

- holding meetings and passing resolutions

- dealing with Companies House.

UNDERSTANDING THE COMPANY'S ARTICLES OF ASSOCIATION

Mention has been made in the previous chapter of the company's **Articles of Association**. It would be as well at this point to explain what these are. The articles are the detailed rules that determine the internal management of the company.

They will normally show amongst other things:

- which clauses of the Companies Act will not apply to the company

- details of how shares are allotted, issued and repurchased

- how share certificates are issued

- how shares are transferred and how the price will be arrived at

- what general meetings are required and for what purpose

- how resolutions and decisions at meetings are to be effected

- the rules governing directors and the secretary

- the limits of the borrowing powers of directors

- the rules for disqualifying directors from holding office

- the extent of indemnity for officials in executing their duties on behalf of the company.

If you do not decide on these for yourself then the standard rules set out in the Companies Act will apply.

APPOINTING YOUR DIRECTORS AND SECRETARY

The directors

The law has given your company a personality but it is really fictitious. It cannot do anything on its own. It is, therefore, essential that it authorises someone to conduct its business for it. Those people authorised are called **directors**.

Officially, directors are appointed to manage the affairs of a company in accordance with its Articles of Association and the law generally. In addition to this a director has responsibilities and these are outlined in Chapter 6.

Note: A director is not officially appointed until form IN01 is submitted to the Registrar of Companies showing details of name, address, date of birth, nationality, occupation and details of any other directorships held (see Figure 12). Subsequent director appointments should be notified on form AP01 (see Figure 6).

Most modern forms of Articles of Association allow any person to be a director. That is, they do not preclude anyone who is barred from being a director by the regulations set out in Table A in the Companies (Tables A to F) Regulations 1985. For example persons over 70 years of age are precluded from being appointed under the regulations in Table A.

These regulations are put in place by the Companies Act to apply if there is no clause in the company's own Articles to overrule them.

Directors will have an equal say in the running of the affairs of the company irrespective of the number of shares they may hold, if they hold any at all. It is not compulsory. Also a director may contract with a supplier of goods or services on behalf of the company or may enter into agreements on behalf of the company. It is, therefore, important to choose fellow directors wisely. They could cost the company a great deal of money.

In accordance with
Section 167 of the
Companies Act 2006.

AP01

Appointment of director

Companies House
for the record

You can use the WebFiling service to file this form online.
Please go to www.companieshouse.gov.uk

✓ **What this form is for**	✗ **What this form is NOT for**	For further information, please
You may use this form to appoint an individual as a director.	You cannot use the form to appoint a corporate director. To do this, please use form AP02 'Appointment of corporate director'.	refer to our guidance at www.companieshouse.gov.uk

1   Company details

Company number	2 9 5 8 1 4 1
Company name in full	SINCLAIR BROOK LTD

→ **Filling in this form**
Please complete in typescript or in bold black capitals.

All fields are mandatory unless specified or indicated by *

2   Date of director's appointment

Date of appointment	ᵈ2 ᵈ1 ᵐ0 ᵐ9 ʸ2 ʸ0 ʸX ʸX

3   New director's details

Title*	MRS
Full forename(s)	EMILY
Surname	BURNS
Former name(s) ❶	
Country/State of residence ❷	ENGLAND
Nationality	BRITISH
Date of birth	ᵈ1 ᵈ9 ᵐ0 ᵐ3 ʸ1 ʸ9 ʸ7 ʸ0
Business occupation (if any) ❸	

❶ **Former name(s)**
Please provide any previous names which have been used for business purposes in the past 20 years.

Married women do not need to give former names unless previously used for business purposes.

Continue in section 6 if required.

❷ **Country/State of residence**
This is in respect of your usual residential address as stated in Section 4a.

❸ **Business occupation**
If you have a business occupation, please enter here. If you do not, please leave blank.

4   New director's service address ❹

Please complete your service address below. You must also complete your usual residential address in **Section 4a**.

Building name/number	THE BARN
Street	RIVER LANE
Post town	HERTFORD
County/Region	HERTS
Postcode	S G 1 4 0 X X
Country	ENGLAND

❹ **Service address**
This is the address that will appear on the public record. This does not have to be your usual residential address.

Please state 'The Company's Registered Office' if your service address is recorded in the company's register of directors as the company's registered office.

If you provide your residential address here it will appear on the public record.

BIS | Department for Business
Innovation & Skills

CHFP000
05/10 Version 4.0

Fig. 6. Appointment of director (Form AP01).

AP01
Appointment of director

Do not cover this barcode

4a	**New director's usual residential address ❶**

	Please complete your usual residential address below.	❶ **New director's usual residential address** Please state 'Same as service address' in this section if your usual residential address is recorded in the company's register of director's residential addresses as 'Same as service address'.
Building name/number	2	
Street	BARONS LANE	
		You cannot state 'Same as service address' if your service address has been stated in Section 4 as 'The Company's Registered Office'. You will need to complete the address in full.
Post town	HERTFORD	
County/Region	HERTS	
Postcode	S G 1 4 0 X X	
Country	ENGLAND	This address cannot be a PO Box, DX or LP (Legal Post in Scotland) number.

Section 243 of Companies Act 2006	**Section 243 exemption ❷**	
	Only tick the box below if you are in the process of applying for, or have been granted, exemption by the Registrar from disclosing your usual residential address to credit reference agencies under section 243 of the Companies Act 2006. ☐ **Different postal address:** If you are applying for, or have been granted, a section 243 exemption, please post this whole form to the different postal address below: The Registrar of Companies, PO Box 4082, Cardiff, CF14 3WE. Where you are applying for a section 243 exemption with this notice, the application and this form must be posted together.	❷ If you are currently in the process of applying for, or have been granted, a section 243 exemption, you may wish to check you have not entered your usual residential address in Section 4 as this will appear on the public record.

CHFP000
05/10 Version 4.0

Fig. 6. (continued).

AP01
Appointment of director

---

5   **Signatures**

I consent to act as director of the above named company.

New director's signature

Signature

X   X

Authorising signature

Signature

X   X

This form may be signed and authorised by:
Director ❶, Secretary, Person authorised ❷, Administrator, Administrative Receiver, Receiver, Receiver manager, Charity commission receiver and manager, CIC manager, Judicial factor.

❶ **Societas Europaea**
If the form is being filed on behalf of a Societas Europaea (SE) please delete 'director' and insert details of which organ of the SE the person signing has membership.

❷ **Person authorised**
Under either section 270 or 274 of the Companies Act 2006.

---

6   **Additional former names** (continued from Section 3)

Former names ❸

❸ **Additional former names**
Use this space to enter any additional names.

Fig. 6. (continued).

AP01
Appointment of director

👤 Presenter information

You do not have to give any contact information, but if you do it will help Companies House if there is a query on the form. The contact information you give will be visible to searchers of the public record.

Contact name

Company name

Address

Post town

County/Region

Postcode

Country

DX

Telephone

✓ Checklist

We may return forms completed incorrectly or with information missing.

Please make sure you have remembered the following:
- ☐ The company name and number match the information held on the public Register.
- ☐ You have provided a business occupation if you have one.
- ☐ You have provided a correct date of birth.
- ☐ You have completed the date of appointment.
- ☐ You have completed the nationality box in Section 3.
- ☐ You have provided both the service address and the usual residential address.
- ☐ Addresses must be a physical location. They cannot be a PO Box number (unless part of a full service address), DX or LP (Legal Post in Scotland) number.
- ☐ You have included all former names used for business purposes over the last 20 years.
- ☐ You have enclosed a relevant section 243 application if applying for this at the same time as completing this form.
- ☐ The new director has signed the form.
- ☐ You have provided an authorising signature.

❗ Important information

Please note that all information on this form will appear on the public record, apart from information relating to usual residential addresses.

✉ Where to send

You may return this form to any Companies House address, however for expediency we advise you to return it to the appropriate address below:

For companies registered in England and Wales:
The Registrar of Companies, Companies House, Crown Way, Cardiff, Wales, CF14 3UZ.
DX 33050 Cardiff.

For companies registered in Scotland:
The Registrar of Companies, Companies House, Fourth floor, Edinburgh Quay 2,
139 Fountainbridge, Edinburgh, Scotland, EH3 9FF.
DX ED235 Edinburgh 1
or LP - 4 Edinburgh 2 (Legal Post).

For companies registered in Northern Ireland:
The Registrar of Companies, Companies House, Second Floor, The Linenhall, 32-38 Linenhall Street, Belfast, Northern Ireland, BT2 8BG.
DX 481 N.R. Belfast 1.

Section 243 exemption
If you are applying for, or have been granted a section 243 exemption, please post this whole form to the different postal address below:
The Registrar of Companies, PO Box 4082, Cardiff, CF14 3WE.

ℹ Further information

For further information please see the guidance notes on the website at www.companieshouse.gov.uk or email enquiries@companieshouse.gov.uk

This form is available in an alternative format. Please visit the forms page on the website at www.companieshouse.gov.uk

This form has been provided free of charge by Companies House.

CHFP000
05/10 Version 4.0

Fig. 6. (continued).

The company secretary

The secretary of a company is the legal guardian of the company. The company secretary sees that the rules and procedures of the company are being adhered to and records all the formal proceedings. A company secretary does not have to be a lawyer but should be someone who appreciates that the law is important and carries out formalities diligently.

The responsibilities of the company secretary include:

- recording minutes of meetings

- maintaining a register of shareholders

- dealing with the formalities of any share dealings.

The company secretary is responsible to the directors. Firms of accountants or solicitors may offer to prepare the formal documents required with the secretary just signing them.

Private companies do not have to appoint a company secretary unless they choose to do so. If a company secretary is appointed the rights and responsibilities will be the same as before. Form AP03 should be completed on appointing a secretary (see Figure 7).

GETTING A REGISTERED OFFICE

Every company must have an official address. This is called the **registered office**.

The purpose of a registered office is to provide an address to which notices and other communications can be sent. The Registrar is notified of the address of the first registered office when Form

In accordance with
Section 276 of the
Companies Act 2006.

AP03

Appointment of secretary

You can use the WebFiling service to file this form online.
Please go to www.companieshouse.gov.uk

✓ **What this form is for**
You may use this form to appoint
an individual as a secretary.

✗ **What this form is NOT for**
You cannot use this form if you are
appointing a corporate secretary.
To do this, please use form
AP04 'Appointment of corporate
secretary'.

For further information, please
refer to our guidance at
www.companieshouse.gov.uk

---

1 **Company details**

Company number	2 9 5 8 1 4 1
Company name in full	

→ **Filling in this form**
Please complete in typescript or in
bold black capitals.

All fields are mandatory unless
specified or indicated by *

---

2 **Date of secretary's appointment**

Date of appointment	0 7 0 4 2 0 X X

---

3 **New secretary's details**

Title*	MISS
Full forename(s)	CAROL
Surname	BIRCH
Former name(s) ❶	

❶ **Former name(s)**
Please provide any previous names
which have been used for business
purposes in the past 20 years.

Married women do not need to give
former names unless previously used
for business purposes.

Continue in section 6 if required.

---

4 **New secretary's service address** ❷

Please complete your service address below.

Building name/number	7
Street	SWANS AVENUE
Post town	HERTFORD
County/Region	HERTS
Postcode	S G 1 4 0 X X
Country	ENGLAND

❷ **Secretary's service address**
This is the address that will
appear on the public record. This
does not have to be your usual
residential address.

Please state 'The Company's
Registered Office' if your service
address is recorded in the company's
register of secretaries as the
company's registered office.

If you provide your residential
address here it will appear on the
public record.

BIS | Department for Business
Innovation & Skills

CHFP000
05/10 Version 4.0

Fig. 7. Appointment of secretary (Form AP03).

AP03
Appointment of secretary

5	**Signatures**	
	I consent to act as secretary of the above named company.	**❶ Societas Europaea** If the form is being filed on behalf of a Societas Europaea (SE) please delete 'director' and insert details of which organ of the SE the person signing has membership.
New secretary's signature	Signature ✗ ✗	
Authorising signature	Signature ✗ ✗	**❷ Person authorised** Under either section 270 or 274 of the Companies Act 2006.
	This form may be signed and authorised by: Director ❶, Secretary, Person authorised ❷, Administrator, Administrative Receiver, Receiver, Receiver manager, Charity commission receiver and manager, CIC manager, Judicial factor.	

6	**Additional former names** (continued from Section 3)	
Former names ❸		**❸ Additional former names** Use this space to enter any additional names.

CHFP000
05/10 Version 4.0

Fig. 7. (continued).

AP03
Appointment of secretary

👤 Presenter information

You do not have to give any contact information, but if you do it will help Companies House if there is a query on the form. The contact information you give will be visible to searchers of the public record.

Contact name

Company name

Address

Post town

County/Region

Postcode

Country

DX

Telephone

✓ Checklist

We may return forms completed incorrectly or with information missing.

Please make sure you have remembered the following:

☐ The company name and number match the information held on the public Register.
☐ You have completed the date of appointment.
☐ You have provided the service address.
☐ The address must be a physical location. It cannot be a PO Box number (unless part of a full address), DX or LP (Legal Post in Scotland) number.
☐ You have included all former names used for business purposes over the last 20 years.
☐ The new secretary has signed the form.
☐ You have provided an authorising signature.

❗ Important information

Please note that all information on this form will appear on the public record.

✉ Where to send

You may return this form to any Companies House address, however for expediency we advise you to return it to the appropriate address below:

For companies registered in England and Wales:
The Registrar of Companies, Companies House,
Crown Way, Cardiff, Wales, CF14 3UZ.
DX 33050 Cardiff.

For companies registered in Scotland:
The Registrar of Companies, Companies House,
Fourth floor, Edinburgh Quay 2,
139 Fountainbridge, Edinburgh, Scotland, EH3 9FF.
DX ED235 Edinburgh 1
or LP - 4 Edinburgh 2 (Legal Post).

For companies registered in Northern Ireland:
The Registrar of Companies, Companies House,
Second Floor, The Linenhall, 32-38 Linenhall Street,
Belfast, Northern Ireland, BT2 8BG.
DX 481 N.R. Belfast 1.

ℹ Further information

For further information, please see the guidance notes on the website at www.companieshouse.gov.uk or email enquiries@companieshouse.gov.uk

This form is available in an alternative format. Please visit the forms page on the website at www.companieshouse.gov.uk

This form has been provided free of charge by Companies House.

CHFP000
05/10 Version 4.0

Fig. 7. (continued).

IN01 is completed (see Figure 12) and submitted at the formation of the company. Any change in the address must be notified to the Registrar within 14 days of the change on form AD01 (see Figure 8). Remember that the **domicile** (e.g. England or Scotland) must remain the same.

Your registered office can be any address. It may be your business address or your home address or it may be the address of your accountant or solicitor. Their permission should, of course, be obtained first.

Any official document, like a writ, can be served on the company at its official registered office and will be deemed to have been delivered to the company. You cannot turn round and make the excuse that it was delivered to your accountant!

DISPLAYING YOUR CERTIFICATE OF INCORPORATION

When your Memorandum and Articles have been registered with the Registrar of Companies he will issue a signed certificate, known as the Certificate of Incorporation (see Figure 2), which is the conclusive evidence that your company is actually in existence in accordance with the Companies Act. You may now commence business.

Your Certificate of Incorporation must be displayed in a prominent position at your principal place of business. There are rules about companies displaying certain information for the benefit of the public at large. This is proof to them that the company is bona fide and that they are trading with a legitimate business.

In accordance with
Section 87 of the
Companies Act 2006.

AD01

Change of registered office address

You can use the WebFiling service to file this form online.
Please go to www.companieshouse.gov.uk

✓ What this form is for	✗ What this form is NOT for	For further information, please
You may use this form to change a company's registered office address.	You cannot use this form to change the registered office address of a Limited Liability Partnership (LLP). To do this, please use form LL AD01's Change of registered office address of a limited liability partnership (LLP).	refer to our guidance at www.companieshouse.gov.uk

1 Company details

Company number	2 9 5 8 1 4 1	→ **Filling in this form** Please complete in typescript or in bold black capitals.
Company name in full	SINCLAIR BROOK LTD	All fields are mandatory unless specified or indicated by *

2 New registered office address ❶

The change in registered office address does not take effect until the Registrar has registered this notice.

A person may validly serve any document on the company at its previous registered office for 14 days from the date that a change of registered office is registered.

❶ **Change of registered office**
For England and Wales companies, the address provided can either be in England or Wales.

For Welsh companies, the address provided must be in Wales.

For companies registered in Scotland or Northern Ireland, the address provided must be in Scotland or Northern Ireland respectively.

Building name/number	UNIT 3, THE GABLES
Street	WELLINGTON STREET
Post town	WARE
County/Region	HERTS
Postcode	S G 1 2 0 X X

3 Signature

I am signing this form on behalf of the company.

Signature	Signature **X**	**X**

This form may be signed by:
Director ❷, Secretary, Person Authorised ❸, Liquidator, Administrator, Administrative receiver, Receiver, Receiver manager, Charity commission receiver and manager, CIC manager, Judicial factor.

❷ **Societas Europaea**
If the form is being filed on behalf of a Societas Europaea (SE), please delete 'director' and insert details of which organ of the SE the person signing has membership.

❸ **Person authorised**
Under either section 270 or 274 of the Companies Act 2006.

Fig. 8. Change of registered office (Form AD01).

AD01

Change of registered office address

✓ Checklist

We may return forms completed incorrectly or with information missing.

Please make sure you have remembered the following:
- ☐ The company name and number match the information held on the public Register.
- ☐ You have provided the new registered office address in section 2.
- ☐ The registered office is in the location where the company was registered e.g. England and Wales, Wales, Scotland, Northern Ireland.
- ☐ You have signed the form.

❗ Important information

Please note that all information on this form will appear on the public record.

✉ Where to send

You may return this form to any Companies House address, however for expediency we advise you to return it to the appropriate address below:

For companies registered in England and Wales:
The Registrar of Companies, Companies House, Crown Way, Cardiff, Wales, CF14 3UZ.
DX 33050 Cardiff.

For companies registered in Scotland:
The Registrar of Companies, Companies House, Fourth floor, Edinburgh Quay 2, 139 Fountainbridge, Edinburgh, Scotland, EH3 9FF.
DX ED235 Edinburgh 1
or LP - 4 Edinburgh 2 (Legal Post).

For companies registered in Northern Ireland:
The Registrar of Companies, Companies House, Second Floor, The Linenhall, 32-38 Linenhall Street, Belfast, Northern Ireland, BT2 8BG.
DX 481 N.R. Belfast 1.

ℹ Further information

For further information, please see the guidance notes on the website at www.companieshouse.gov.uk or email enquiries@companieshouse.gov.uk

This form is available in an alternative format. Please visit the forms page on the website at www.companieshouse.gov.uk

This form has been provided free of charge by Companies House.

CHFP000
05/10 Version 4.0

Fig. 8. (continued).

HOLDING MEETINGS AND PASSING RESOLUTIONS

Holding meetings

You are now aware that the ultimate responsibility for the conduct of any company lies with the shareholders, even though the directors make most of the management decisions.

It is therefore necessary for a company to give its shareholders a platform from which to exercise their responsibility. This is usually in the form of a meeting and may be:

- the company's annual general meeting (AGM)

- an extraordinary general meeting (EGM)

- any general meeting called for a specific purpose (SGM)

There are strict rules governing meetings and these are normally contained in the Articles of Association. These will cover:

- how the Chairman of the meeting will be appointed

- how many members (shareholders) must be present for the meeting to transact any business (this is known as a **quorum**)

- how much notice must be given to each member that such a meeting is going to take place.

However, it is no longer necessary to hold an AGM.

Shareholders' first meeting

It will be advantageous to hold a meeting as soon as the company has been incorporated. This will establish the ground rules for operation of the company and leave no room for doubt later.

The minutes of this meeting will contain the name of the company, its company number, the subscribers of shares, where the registered address is, and the full Memorandum and Articles of Association as amended by the shareholders where applicable.

Any company must define what it is and what it is for. This is done in a document known as the Memorandum of Association, which states the name of the company and lists each subscriber who wishes to become a member and agrees to take at least one share. It is a very comprehensive document that states not only the name of the company, but where it is situated (i.e. which country), and its main objects.

Examples of a Memorandum of Association (Figure 10) and Articles of Association (Figure 11) are shown below, along with minutes of the meeting (Figure 9) at which these items were approved.

The Chairman of a meeting will normally be the chairman of the company or the principal shareholder. However, it is customary that the Articles will allow for any member present at the meeting to be elected Chairman.

In general there must be two people present to constitute a meeting unless the Articles provide for a different number. Directors may call general meetings, including the annual general meeting, by giving required notice. In addition members may, in accordance with the Companies Act, require the directors to convene an extraordinary general meeting.

These formal meetings are held when important matters relating to the running of the company are to be discussed and, if necessary, voted upon.

First Minutes
of
Brook Sinclair Ltd

Certificate Number: 2958141

PRESENT: Mathew Browning, Simon Browning, and Leesa Browning

At a Meeting of the Board of Directors of Sinclair Brook Limited, it was unanimously noted on the 12ᵗʰ August 20XX that:

CERTIFICATE OF INCORPORATION: The Company's Certificate of Incorporation Number is: 2958141 dated the 12 August 20XX.

DOCUMENTS FILED PRIOR TO INCORPORATION: Pursuant to the Companies Acts of 1985 and 1989 the electronic equivalent to Government Forms G10 and G12 were lodged with Companies House showing that the First Directors were Amersham Services Limited and Pemex Services Limited and that the Company Secretary was Pemex Services Limited.

SUBSCRIBERS: That the subscribers to the Memorandum & Articles of Association were:

Mathew Browning	600 ORDINARY SHARES
Leesa Browning	200 ORDINARY SHARES
Simon Browning	200 ORDINARY SHARES

REGISTERED OFFICE ADDRESS: The registered office address of the company is ENGLAND

THERE BEING NO FURTHER BUSINESS THE MEETING CONCLUDED.

CHAIRPERSON: DATED: 12 AUGUST 20XX

Fig. 9. First minutes.

THE COMPANIES ACT 1985
COMPANY LIMITED BY SHARES
MEMORANDUM OF ASSOCIATION
OF
Sinclair Brook
LIMITED

(1) THE COMPANY'S NAME IS: Sinclair Brook LIMITED

(2) THE COMPANY'S REGISTERED OFFICE IS TO BE LOCATED IN ENGLAND

(3) THE COMPANY'S OBJECTS ARE:

  (a) To carry out any and/or all business activities including but not limited to retail and wholesale activities, general consultancy, import and/or export and/or distribution of any and/or all goods and/or services and/or any other business activities deemed to be in the interests of the Company by the Board of Directors whether or not ancillary and/or complimentary to any other activities provided that such activities are lawful under the laws of England & Wales [or Scotland].

  (b) To purchase or otherwise acquire any interest in real or personal property including: easements, rights of way, concessions, licences, mortgages, leases, or to sell, hire, rent, surrender or accept surrender, or otherwise deal with freehold, leasehold or any other legal title, or to purchase or otherwise acquire plant and/or machinery, patents, industrial and/or commercial processes as is adjudged by the board to be in the interests of the company.

  (c) To erect, build, manufacture, construct, adapt, alter, let or hire, remodel, repair, assemble, pull down, dismantle, enlarge, remove or replace any: shops, stores, offices, warehouses, factories, railways, office equipment, factory plant and material, roads, pathways, or anything else which may be advantageous or convenient to the Company and to subsidise or make such contribution, either directly or indirectly, or to maintain any of the above in anyway deemed to be in the best interests of the Company by the Board of Directors.

  (d) To act as wholesaler, retailer or purchaser, sell, import or export any goods, services or property, and to give such undertakings, guarantees, part-exchanges as are appropriate in the circumstances and that will be in the best interest of the Company as adjudged by the Board of Directors.

  (e) To borrow or raise money or ensure such facilities in connection with the Company's business with such security and at such interest rates as may be considered expedient in all the circumstances. In particular the aforementioned can be secured by: mortgage, charge, bond, by

Fig. 10. Memorandum of Association.

using the uncalled capital of the Company, the issue of shares either at par, market or discount value, with such terms, preferences and privileges as are considered appropriate, the issue of debentures, either permanent, repayable or redeemable and further by, or separately to the above, any trust deed or other legal assurance which is acceptable to any individual, bank, finance house, company, building society or other legitimate lending body.

(f) To provide credit, act as a guarantor, and/or advance money to customers, firms, companies and others, with or without security, and on such terms as may be deemed appropriate, and to ensure that such advances/guarantees will be honoured if the agreed terms have been satisfied.

(g) To receive money or deposit or loan, on such terms as the Company may agree and to generally act as bankers to firms, companies, customers and others.

(h) To grant pensions, allowances, gratuities and bonuses to officers, ex-officers, employees or the ex-employees of the Company, its subsidiaries, or predecessors, or the dependants of such persons, and to establish and maintain or concur in the upkeep of trusts, funds or schemes (whether contributory or non-contributory) for the purpose of providing pensions and funds for the aforesaid and their dependants.

(i) To draw, make, accept, endorse, discount, execute and issue negotiable or transferable instruments of all kinds including bills of exchange and promissory notes.

(j) To invest and deal with money not immediately required by the Company for its business to be invested in other areas to be determined by the Company as deemed appropriate in the circumstances by the Board of Directors.

(k) To purchase or otherwise acquire all or any part of the business or assets of any person, firm or company formed to carry on, or possessed of such real or personal property rights suitable for the purposes of the Company, and to pay for such in cash (by instalments or otherwise), securities, fully or partly paid up shares or by any other method, on such terms and for such time period thought suitable.

(l) To accept payment for any property or rights disposed of by the Company on such terms and by such method as seems suitable in the circumstances including the right to accept stock/shares in another company or corporation, with or without preferential rights, debentures, mortgage debentures or any other security approved by the Company.

(m) To amalgamate, co-operate, come to an arrangement or partnership with any firm, company or person that may benefit the business of this Company, and on such terms and for such time period as may be approved and to acquire, sell, hold or dispose of any real or personal property, shares, stocks or other interests in any such body and to guarantee the contracts or liabilities of and/or assist such, in keeping with the approval terms.

Fig. 10. (continued).

(n)   To sell and in any other manner deal with or dispose of the Company or any of the property, rights and assets, for such consideration and on such terms that may be approved, including the right to manage, improve, turn to account, exchange, rent, have a share of profits or to grant licences, easements, privileges or other such interests and to acquire and protect and renew trade marks, patents, licences, concessions and designs.

(o)   To pay all and any expenses incurred in connection with the promotion, function, formation and incorporation of this Company.

(p)   To distribute any property in specie among any members of the Company. To do all or any of the aforementioned in any part of the world as principals, agents, trustees, contractors or otherwise, either alone or with others either by or through agents, trustees or otherwise.

(q)   To do all other things that are incidental or conducive to the attainment of the above rights.

It is hereby expressly declared that each of the foregoing paragraphs shall be construed independently of the other paragraphs hereof, and that none of the objects mentioned in any paragraph shall be deemed to be merely subsidiary to the objects mentioned in any of the other paragraphs.

(4)   THE LIABILITY OF THE MEMBERS IS LIMITED.

(5)   THE COMPANY'S SHARE CAPITAL IS £1,000 DIVIDED INTO 1,000 SHARES OF £1.00 EACH.

We, the subscribers and whose Names & Addresses appear herein, wish to be formed into a Limited Company in pursuance of this Memorandum & Articles of Association and agree to take the number of shares in the capital of the Undertaking set opposite our names:

NAME & ADDRESS OF SUBSCRIBERS

MATTHEW BROWNING	600 ORDINARY SHARES
LEESA BROWNING	200 ORDINARY SHARES
SIMON BROWNING	200 ORDINARY SHARES
TOTAL SHARES TAKEN	1,000 ORDINARY SHARES

Fig. 10. (continued).

THE COMPANIES ACT 1985
COMPANY LIMITED BY SHARES
ARTICLES OF ASSOCIATION
OF
SINCLAIR BROOK
Limited

1. Save as otherwise indicated, the regulations contained or incorporated in Table A in the Companies (Tables A to F) Regulations 1985 (hereinafter referred to as 'Table A') shall apply to the Company.
2. Regulations 8, 64, 76, 77 and 113 of Table A shall not apply to the Company.
3. The Company is a private company and accordingly no offer or invitation shall be made to the public (whether for cash or otherwise) to subscribe for shares in or debentures of the Company, nor shall the Company allot or agree to allot (whether for cash or otherwise) any shares in or debentures of the Company with a view to all or any of those shares or debentures being offered for sale to the public.
4. At the date of the adoption of these Articles the capital of the Company is £1,000 divided into 1,000 ordinary shares of £1.00 each.

CAPITAL

5. Subject to Article 6 hereof, the Directors of the Company shall within a period of not more than 5 years from the date of the incorporation, have the authority to exercise the Company's power to allot, grant options over or otherwise deal with or dispose of any relevant securities (as defined by S.80 (2) of the Companies Act, 1985) of the Company to such persons and as such items and conditions that the Directors deem appropriate.
6. (a) Sections 89(1), 90(1) to (6) of the Companies Act 1985 shall not apply in relation to the issue of any equity securities by the Company but are substituted by Article 6 (subparagraph b) hereof.
   (b) Save as otherwise directed by the Company in a general meeting all shares allotted pursuant to Article 5 hereof must first be offered to the members of the Company in as near a proportion as possible to the existing shares held by them and that such offer shall be made by notice in writing stating the number of shares to which each member is entitled and limiting a time period of not less than 21 days for the offer to be accepted. If such offer is not accepted it will be deemed to have been declined and the Directors may, subject to these Articles, allot or otherwise dispose of the said shares in a manner that they deem most beneficial to the interests of the Company. If, however, the Directors are of the opinion that the shares cannot be conveniently offered to the members as hereinbefore provided they may otherwise dispose, allot, or grant options over the same to such persons and on such terms as they think appropriate.

Fig. 11. Articles of Association.

LIEN

7. The lien conferred by Regulation 8 Table A of the Companies Act 1985 on shares and dividends shall also apply to fully paid up shares and dividends registered in the name of any person in respect of all money owed by such person to the Company on whatever basis, whether he is the sole registered holder or one or two or more thereof, or however held.

TRANSFER OF SHARES

8. Without assigning any reason the Directors may, with absolute discretion, decline to register any transfer of any share or shares whether or not, it or they, are fully paid up. The first sentence of Regulation 24 of Table A of the Companies Act 1985 is accordingly not applicable.

PROCEEDINGS AT GENERAL MEETINGS

9. There shall appear with reasonable prominence a statement that a member entitled to attend and vote is entitled to appoint a proxy to attend and vote instead of him and that a proxy need not be a member of the company (S.372 (3) of the Companies Act 1985 with Regulation 38 of Table A modified and the second sentence of Regulation 59 of Table A to be deleted).

DIRECTORS

10. There must be at least one Director but no maximum number of Directors unless and until decided by the Company in a general meeting. If there is a sole Director such director will have all the powers and authorities granted by these Articles and Table A of the Companies Act 1985 as if there were two or more Directors with Regulations 89 and 90 modified accordingly. The first Directors of the Company shall be the person or persons named in the statement to the Registrar of Companies prior to the formation of the Company pursuant to S.10 of the Companies Act 1985, and such Directors need not hold shares in the Company but shall, nevertheless, be entitled to receive notice and attend all the meetings of the Company.

11. The Company shall not be subject to S.293 of the Companies Act 1985 and, therefore, any person can be appointed or elected as a Director, whatever his age and no Director shall be required to vacate his Directorship by reason of his attaining or having attained the age of 70 years.

12. No Director shall be subject to retirement by rotation and a Director can only be elected at a general meeting unless:

(a) he is recommended by the Directors; or

(b) not less than 15 or more than 35 days before the date of the meeting notice has been given to the Company of the intention to propose that person for election, together with a notice in writing signed by that person of his willingness to be elected.

Fig. 11. (continued).

The **annual general meeting** (AGM) is normally used as a reporting meeting to give the shareholders a résumé of the year's events and results and to present the accounts for the preceding financial year.

An **extraordinary general meeting** is usually called where there is a dispute to be settled, but in very small companies this is more likely to be a personality clash and will probably not be resolved by a formal meeting.

Passing resolutions

Decisions are taken at meetings by passing **resolutions**.

What is a resolution?

It is an agreement by those entitled to vote at a meeting on any lawful matter brought before it. A proposed resolution is called a motion. When a motion is passed the company is bound by it until circumstances alter or another motion is passed superseding it. If the necessary majority of votes is not obtained the motion fails.

There are a number of different types of resolution.

Directors' resolutions

These are used at directors' board meetings and for normal management business. They are not normally required to be filed with the Registrar of Companies, but a record should be kept so that the content may be referred to at a later date in the event of a difference of opinion.

Ordinary resolutions

These are passed by a simple majority of the votes cast and are used for matters not requiring another type of resolution. Unless otherwise stated all resolutions are ordinary resolutions. A **proxy** (someone to vote on your behalf) may be allowed in some circumstances.

Private companies may resolve problems by written resolution without a meeting being held and without formal notice provided it is a matter which could be passed by the company in general meeting. However, the resolution can only be passed by the unanimous agreement of all those members who would be entitled to attend and vote at such a meeting. The date of this resolution would be the date the last person signed.

These resolutions must also be sent to the auditors.

Elective resolutions

These are a type of resolution brought in by the Companies Act 1989. They must be used in private companies only and must have unanimous support of the members. They are used for five specific purposes:

1. To alter the duration of the authority of directors to allot securities.

2. To dispense with the holding of annual general meetings.

3. To dispense with the laying of accounts and reports before the members in general meeting.

4. To reduce the majority required to authorise short notice of a meeting and notice of a resolution from 95 per cent to not less than 90 per cent.

5. To dispense with the annual appointment of auditors.

Very few private company resolutions have to be sent to the Registrar of Companies for filing. Those which do are specified by the Companies Acts and include all special, extraordinary and elective resolutions. These must be filed within 15 days of them being passed.

Example of elective resolution

It was resolved that in accordance with the provisions of the Companies Act the company hereby dispenses with the holding of the Annual General Meeting for 20XX and subsequent years.

DEALING WITH COMPANIES HOUSE

It will be apparent by now that the Registrar of Companies requires private companies to keep him/her informed on certain matters. Companies are, to that extent, public property and the files are available for public inspection.

It is the duty of the directors and the job of the company secretary to submit various forms and resolutions to Companies House within prescribed time limits. The penalty for not doing so is normally a hefty fine. In extreme circumstances the company can be struck off the register.

It is in your interest to fulfil your obligations as people who deal with you can easily lose confidence in you as a businessperson if you do not.

Statutory information to be sent to the Registrar includes:

■ changes to the registered office

■ changes of directors and secretary or their particulars

■ annual returns

- copies of extraordinary, elective and special resolutions

- details of any mortgages or charges on the company property

- resolutions to change the Memorandum and Articles

- notification that the company has gone into liquidation or receivership.

ACTION POINTS AND REMINDERS

1. Ask your company formation agent for a sight of the Articles of Association before he completes the registration.

2. Decide who your directors will be.

3. Decide how many shares you will issue to each.

4. Ensure that your company secretary knows what obligations the post carries.

5. Do you have the address of your registered office organised?

6. Where will you display your certificate of incorporation?

7. Where will you hold official company meetings?

8. Will you insist on being chairman yourself?

9. Appreciate that you are responsible for statutory information being sent to the Registrar.

Completing Your
Application

4

Now that you have decided on your business, its name, its shareholders, its directors and secretary (if you have one) you are now ready to complete form IN01 and submit it to the Registrar.

The form seems a formidable document at 18 pages, but it is reproduced here in Figure 12 in its entirety for information purposes.

A small private company, limited by shares, will only have to complete parts of the form and the instructions are simple to follow.

In accordance with
Section 9 of the
Companies Act 2006.

IN01

Application to register a company

A fee is payable with this form.
Please see 'How to pay' on the last page.

✓ **What this form is for**	✗ **What this form is NOT for**	For further information, please
You may use this form to register a private or public company.	You cannot use this form to register a limited liability partnership. To do this, please use form LL IN01.	refer to our guidance at www.companieshouse.gov.uk

---

Part 1   Company details

→ **Filling in this form**
Please complete in typescript or in bold black capitals.

All fields are mandatory unless specified or indicated by *

A1	**Company details**

Please show the proposed company name below.

Proposed company name in full ❶

SINCLAIR BROOK LTD

For official use

❶ **Duplicate names**
Duplicate names are not permitted. A list of registered names can be found on our website. There are various rules that may affect your choice of name. More information is available at: www.companieshouse.gov.uk

A2	**Company name restrictions ❷**

Please tick the box only if the proposed company name contains sensitive or restricted words or expressions that require you to seek comments of a government department or other specified body.

☐ I confirm that the proposed company name contains sensitive or restricted words or expressions and that approval, where appropriate, has been sought of a government department or other specified body and I attach a copy of their response.

❷ **Company name restrictions**
A list of sensitive or restricted words or expressions that require consent can be found in guidance available on our website: www.companieshouse.gov.uk

A3	**Exemption from name ending with 'Limited' or 'Cyfyngedig' ❸**

Please tick the box if you wish to apply for exemption from the requirement to have the name ending with 'Limited', Cyfyngedig' or permitted alternative.

☐ I confirm that the above proposed company meets the conditions for exemption from the requirement to have a name ending with 'Limited', 'Cyfyngedig' or permitted alternative.

❸ **Name ending exemption**
Only private companies that are limited by guarantee and meet other specific requirements are eligible to apply for this.
For more details, please go to our website: www.companieshouse.gov.uk

A4	**Company type❹**

Please tick the box that describes the proposed company type and members' liability (only one box must be ticked):

☐ Public limited by shares
☑ Private limited by shares
☐ Private limited by guarantee
☐ Private unlimited with share capital
☐ Private unlimited without share capital

❹ **Company type**
If you are unsure of your company's type, please go to our website: www.companieshouse.gov.uk

BIS | Department for Business Innovation & Skills

CHFP000
04/11 Version 4.1

Fig. 12. Application to register a company (Form IN01).

IN01
Application to register a company

A5   **Situation of registered office** ❶

Please tick the appropriate box below that describes the situation of the proposed registered office (only one box must be ticked): ☐ England and Wales ☐ Wales ☐ Scotland ☐ Northern Ireland	**❶ Registered office** Every company must have a registered office and this is the address to which the Registrar will send correspondence. For England and Wales companies, the address must be in England or Wales. For Welsh, Scottish or Northern Ireland companies, the address must be in Wales, Scotland or Northern Ireland respectively.

A6   **Registered office address** ❷

Please give the registered office address of your company.

Building name/number	PELICAN HOUSE
Street	HIGH STREET
Post town	WARE
County/Region	HERTS
Postcode	S G 1 2 0 X X

❷ Registered office address
You must ensure that the address shown in this section is consistent with the situation indicated in section A5.

You must provide an address in England or Wales for companies to be registered in England and Wales.

You must provide an address in Wales, Scotland or Northern Ireland for companies to be registered in Wales, Scotland or Northern Ireland respectively.

A7   **Articles of association** ❸

Please choose one option only and tick one box only.

Option 1   I wish to adopt one of the following model articles in its entirety. Please tick only **one** box.

☑ Private limited by shares
☐ Private limited by guarantee
☐ Public company

Option 2   I wish to adopt the following model articles with additional and/or amended provisions. I attach a copy of the additional and/or amended provision(s). Please tick only **one** box.

☐ Private limited by shares
☐ Private limited by guarantee
☐ Public company

Option 3   ☐ I wish to adopt entirely bespoke articles. I attach a copy of the bespoke articles to this application.

❸ For details of which company type can adopt which model articles, please go to our website: www.companieshouse.gov.uk

---

A8   **Restricted company articles** ❹

Please tick the box below if the company's articles are restricted.

☐

❹ Restricted company articles
Restricted company articles are those containing provision for entrenchment. For more details, please go to our website: www.companieshouse.gov.uk

CHFP000
04/11 Version 4.1

Fig. 12. (continued).

Part 2   Proposed officers

For private companies the appointment of a secretary is optional, however, if you do decide to appoint a company secretary you must provide the relevant details. Public companies are required to appoint at least one secretary.

Private companies must appoint at least one director who is an individual. Public companies must appoint at least two directors, one of which must be an individual.

For a secretary who is an individual, go to Section B1; For a corporate secretary, go to Section C1; For a director who is an individual, go to Section D1; For a corporate director, go to Section E1.

Secretary

B1   **Secretary appointments ❶**

Please use this section to list all the secretary appointments taken on formation. **For a corporate secretary, complete Sections C1-C5.**

Title*	MRS
Full forename(s)	LEESA
Surname	BROWNING
Former name(s) ❷	

❶ **Corporate appointments**
For corporate secretary appointments, please complete section C1-C5 instead of section B.

Additional appointments
If you wish to appoint more than one secretary, please use the 'Secretary appointments' continuation page.

❷ **Former name(s)**
Please provide any previous names which have been used for business purposes in the last 20 years. Married women do not need to give former names unless previously used for business purposes.

B2   **Secretary's service address ❸**

Building name/number	21
Street	COLE GREEN ROAD
Post town	HERTFORD
County/Region	HERTS
Postcode	S G 1 4 0 X X
Country	

❸ **Service address**
This is the address that will appear on the public record. This does not have to be your usual residential address.

Please state 'The Company's Registered Office' if your service address will be recorded in the proposed company's register of secretaries as the company's registered office.

If you provide your residential address here it will appear on the public record.

B3   **Signature ❹**

I consent to act as secretary of the proposed company named in **Section A1.**

Signature	Signature X X

❹ **Signature**
The person named above consents to act as secretary of the proposed company.

CHFP000
04/11 Version 4.1

Fig. 12. (continued).

IN01
Application to register a company

Corporate secretary

C1 | Corporate secretary appointments ❶

Please use this section to list all the corporate secretary appointments taken on formation.

Name of corporate body/firm	
Building name/number	
Street	
Post town	
County/Region	
Postcode	
Country	

❶ **Additional appointments**
If you wish to appoint more than one corporate secretary, please use the 'Corporate secretary appointments' continuation page.

Registered or principal address
This is the address that will appear on the public record. This address must be a physical location for the delivery of documents. It cannot be a PO box number (unless contained within a full address), DX number or LP (Legal Post in Scotland) number.

C2 | Location of the registry of the corporate body or firm

Is the corporate secretary registered within the European Economic Area (EEA)?

→ Yes Complete **Section C3 only**
→ No   Complete **Section C4 only**

C3 | EEA companies ❷

Please give details of the register where the company file is kept (including the relevant state) and the registration number in that register.

Where the company/firm is registered ❸	
Registration number	

❷ **EEA**
A full list of countries of the EEA can be found in our guidance:
www.companieshouse.gov.uk

❸ This is the register mentioned in Article 3 of the First Company Law Directive (68/151/EEC).

C4 | Non-EEA companies

Please give details of the legal form of the corporate body or firm and the law by which it is governed. If applicable, please also give details of the register in which it is entered (including the state) and its registration number in that register.

Legal form of the corporate body or firm	
Governing law	
If applicable, where the company/firm is registered ❹	
Registration number	

❹ **Non-EEA**
Where you have provided details of the register (including state) where the company or firm is registered, you must also provide its number in that register.

C5 | Signature ❺

I consent to act as secretary of the proposed company named in **Section A1.**

Signature	Signature X X

❺ **Signature**
The person named above consents to act as corporate secretary of the proposed company.

CHFP000
04/11 Version 4.1

Fig. 12. (continued).

IN01

Application to register a company

Director

D1 — Director appointments ❶

Please use this section to list all the director appointments taken on formation.
For a corporate director, complete Sections E1-E5.

Title*	MR
Full forename(s)	MATHEW
Surname	BROWNING
Former name(s) ❷	
Country/State of residence ❸	ENGLAND
Nationality	BRITISH
Date of birth	$^d0$ $^d8$ $^m0$ $^m7$ $^y1$ $^y9$ $^y6$ $^y4$
Business occupation (if any) ❺	FINANCIAL CONSULTANT

❶ Appointments
Private companies must appoint at least one director who is an individual. Public companies must appoint at least two directors, one of which must be an individual.

❷ Former name(s)
Please provide any previous names which have been used for business purposes in the last 20 years. Married women do not need to give former names unless previously used for business purposes.

❸ Country/State of residence
This is in respect of your usual residential address as stated in section D4.

❺ Business occupation
If you have a business occupation, please enter here. If you do not, please leave blank.

Additional appointments
If you wish to appoint more than one director, please use the 'Director appointments' continuation page.

D2 — Director's service address ❻

Please complete the service address below. You must also fill in the director's usual residential address in **Section D4.**

Building name/number	27
Street	HAILEYBURY STREET
Post town	MELBOURN
County/Region	HERTS
Postcode	S G 2 7	8 K K
Country	ENGLAND

❻ Service address
This is the address that will appear on the public record. This does not have to be your usual residential address.

Please state 'The Company's Registered Office' if your service address will be recorded in the proposed company's register of directors as the company's registered office.

If you provide your residential address here it will appear on the public record.

D3 — Signature ❼

I consent to act as director of the proposed company named in **Section A1.**

Signature	Signature X X

❼ Signature
The person named above consents to act as director of the proposed company.

CHFP000
04/11 Version 4.1

Fig. 12. (continued).

IN01
Application to register a company

This page is not shown on the public record

Do not cover this barcode

D4 | **Director's usual residential address** ❶

Please complete your usual residential address below.

Building name/number	88
Street	YARRA STREET
Post town	MELBOURN
County/Region	HERTS
Postcode	M E 4 9 0 X X
Country	ENGLAND

❶ **New director's usual residential address**
Please state 'Same as service address' in this section If your usual residential address is recorded in the company's proposed register of director's residential addresses as 'Same as service address'.

You cannot state 'Same as service address' if your service address has been stated in Section D2 as 'The Company's Registered Office'. You will need to complete the address in full.

This address cannot be a PO Box, DX or LP (Legal Post in Scotland) number.

Section 243 of Companies Act 2006

Section 243 exemption ❷

Only tick the box below if you are in the process of applying for, or have been granted, exemption by the Registrar from disclosing your usual residential address to credit reference agencies under section 243 of the Companies Act 2006.

☐

Different postal address:
If you are applying for, or have been granted, a section 243 exemption, please post this whole form to the different postal address below:
The Registrar of Companies, PO Box 4082, Cardiff, CF14 3WE.

Where you are applying for a section 243 exemption with this notice, the application and this form must be posted together.

❷ If you are currently in the process of applying for, or have been granted, a section 243 exemption, you may wish to check you have not entered your usual residential address in Section D2 as this will appear on the public record.

CHFP000
04/11 Version 4.1

Fig. 12. (continued).

IN01
Application to register a company

Director

D1   Director appointments ❶

Please use this section to list all the director appointments taken on formation.
For a corporate director, complete Sections E1-E5.

Title*	MR
Full forename(s)	SIMON
Surname	BROWNING
Former name(s) ❷	
Country/State of residence ❸	ENGLAND
Nationality	BRITISH
Date of birth	$^d0$ $^d1$ $^m1$ $^m2$ $^y1$ $^y9$ $^y6$ $^y2$
Business occupation (if any) ❹	FUNERAL DIRECTOR

❶ **Appointments**
Private companies must appoint at least one director who is an individual. Public companies must appoint at least two directors, one of which must be an individual.

❷ **Former name(s)**
Please provide any previous names which have been used for business purposes in the last 20 years. Married women do not need to give former names unless previously used for business purposes.

❸ **Country/State of residence**
This is in respect of your usual residential address as stated in Section D4.

❹ **Business occupation**
If you have a business occupation, please enter here. If you do not, please leave blank.

Additional appointments
If you wish to appoint more than one director, please use the 'Director appointments' continuation page.

D2   Director's service address ❺

Please complete the service address below. You must also fill in the director's usual residential address in **Section D4.**

Building name/number	62
Street	FARMERS ROAD
Post town	BRAUGHING
County/Region	HERTS
Postcode	S G 1 7 0 X X
Country	

❺ **Service address**
This is the address that will appear on the public record. This does not have to be your usual residential address.

Please state 'The Company's Registered Office' if your service address will be recorded in the proposed company's register of directors as the company's registered office.

If you provide your residential address here it will appear on the public record.

D3   Signature ❻

I consent to act as director of the proposed company named in **Section A1.**

Signature	Signature **X** **X**

❻ **Signature**
The person named above consents to act as director of the proposed company.

CHFP000
04/11 Version 4.1

Fig. 12. (continued).

IN01

Application to register a company

Do not cover this barcode

D4   **Director's usual residential address ❶**

Please complete your usual residential address below.

Building name/number	16
Street	WHITEPIT ROAD
Post town	NEWPORT
County/Region	HERTS
Postcode	N E 2 0 X X
Country	

❶ **New director's usual residential address**
Please state 'Same as service address' in this section if your usual residential address is recorded in the company's proposed register of director's residential addresses as 'Same as service address'.

You cannot state 'Same as service address' if your service address has been stated in section D2 as 'The Company's Registered Office'. You will need to complete the address in full.

This address cannot be a PO Box, DX or LP (Legal Post in Scotland) number.

Section 243 of
Companies Act 2006

Section 243 exemption ❷

Only tick the box below if you are in the process of applying for, or have been granted, exemption by the Registrar from disclosing your usual residential address to credit reference agencies under section 243 of the Companies Act 2006.

☐

Different postal address:
If you are applying for, or have been granted, a section 243 exemption, please post this whole form to the different postal address below:
The Registrar of Companies, PO Box 4082, Cardiff, CF14 3WE.

Where you are applying for a section 243 exemption with this notice, the application and this form must be posted together.

❷ If you are currently in the process of applying for, or have been granted, a section 243 exemption, you may wish to check you have not entered your usual residential address in Section D2 as this will appear on the public record.

Fig. 12. (continued).

IN01
Application to register a company

Corporate director

E1 — Corporate director appointments ❶

Please use this section to list all the corporate directors taken on formation.

Name of corporate body or firm	
Building name/number	
Street	
Post town	
County/Region	
Postcode	
Country	

❶ **Additional appointments**
If you wish to appoint more than one corporate director, please use the 'Corporate director appointments' continuation page.

Registered or principal address
This is the address that will appear on the public record. This address must be a physical location for the delivery of documents. It cannot be a PO box number (unless contained within a full address), DX number or LP (Legal Post in Scotland) number.

E2 — Location of the registry of the corporate body or firm

Is the corporate director registered within the European Economic Area (EEA)?

→ Yes   Complete **Section E3 only**
→ No   Complete **Section E4 only**

E3 — EEA companies ❷

Please give details of the register where the company file is kept (including the relevant state) and the registration number in that register.

Where the company/firm is registered ❸	
Registration number	

❷ **EEA**
A full list of countries of the EEA can be found in our guidance:
www.companieshouse.gov.uk

❸ This is the register mentioned in Article 3 of the First Company Law Directive (68/151/EEC).

E4 — Non-EEA companies

Please give details of the legal form of the corporate body or firm and the law by which it is governed. If applicable, please also give details of the register in which it is entered (including the state) and its registration number in that register.

Legal form of the corporate body or firm	
Governing law	
If applicable, where the company/firm is registered ❹	
If applicable, the registration number	

❹ **Non-EEA**
Where you have provided details of the register (including state) where the company or firm is registered, you must also provide its number in that register.

E5 — Signature ❺

I consent to act as director of the proposed company named in **Section A1**.

Signature	
Signature	Signature X X

❺ **Signature**
The person named above consents to act as corporate director of the proposed company.

CHFP000
04/11 Version 4.1

Fig. 12. (continued).

Part 3 Statement of capital

Does your company have share capital?
- → **Yes** Complete the sections below.
- → **No** Go to **Part 4 (Statement of guarantee).**

F1 **Share capital in pound sterling (£)**

Please complete the table below to show each class of shares held in pound sterling.
If all your issued capital is in sterling, only complete **Section F1** and then go to **Section F4.**

Class of shares (E.g. Ordinary/Preference etc.)	Amount paid up on each share ❶	Amount (if any) unpaid on each share ❶	Number of shares ❷	Aggregate nominal value ❸
ORDINARY	£1		1000	£ 1000
				£
				£
				£
		Totals		£

F2 **Share capital in other currencies**

Please complete the table below to show any class of shares held in other currencies.
Please complete a separate table for each currency.

Currency

Class of shares (E.g. Ordinary/Preference etc.)	Amount paid up on each share ❶	Amount (if any) unpaid on each share ❶	Number of shares ❷	Aggregate nominal value ❸
		Totals		

Currency

Class of shares (E.g. Ordinary/Preference etc.)	Amount paid up on each share ❶	Amount (if any) unpaid on each share ❶	Number of shares ❷	Aggregate nominal value ❸
		Totals		

F3 **Totals**

Please give the total number of shares and total aggregate nominal value of issued share capital.

Total number of shares	1000
Total aggregate nominal value ❹	£1000

❹ **Total aggregate nominal value**
Please list total aggregate values in different currencies separately. For example: £100 + €100 + $10 etc.

❶ Including both the nominal value and any share premium.

❷ Total number of issued shares in this class.

❸ Number of shares issued multiplied by nominal value of each share.

Continuation Pages
Please use a Statement of Capital continuation page if necessary.

Fig. 12. (continued).

IN01
Application to register a company

F4

Statement of capital (Prescribed particulars of rights attached to shares)

Please give the prescribed particulars of rights attached to shares for each class of share shown in the statement of capital share tables in **Sections F1** and **F2**.

Class of share

Prescribed particulars ❶

❶ **Prescribed particulars of rights attached to shares**

The particulars are:
a. particulars of any voting rights, including rights that arise only in certain circumstances;
b. particulars of any rights, as respects dividends, to participate in a distribution;
c. particulars of any rights, as respects capital, to participate in a distribution (including on winding up); and
d. whether the shares are to be redeemed or are liable to be redeemed at the option of the company or the shareholder and any terms or conditions relating to redemption of these shares.

A separate table must be used for each class of share.

Continuation pages
Please use the next page or a 'Statement of Capital (Prescribed particulars of rights attached to shares)' continuation page if necessary.

CHFP000
04/11 Version 4.1

Fig. 12. (continued).

IN01
Application to register a company

Class of share	
Prescribed particulars ❶	

❶ **Prescribed particulars of rights attached to shares**

The particulars are:
a. particulars of any voting rights, including rights that arise only in certain circumstances;
b. particulars of any rights, as respects dividends, to participate in a distribution;
c. particulars of any rights, as respects capital, to participate in a distribution (including on winding up); and
d. whether the shares are to be redeemed or are liable to be redeemed at the option of the company or the shareholder and any terms or conditions relating to redemption of these shares.

A separate table must be used for each class of share.

Continuation pages
Please use a 'Statement of capital (Prescribed particulars of rights attached to shares)' continuation page if necessary.

CHFP000
04/11 Version 4.1

Fig. 12. (continued).

IN01

Application to register a company

Initial shareholdings

This section should only be completed by companies incorporating with share capital.

Please complete the details below for each subscriber.

The addresses will appear on the public record. These do not need to be the subscribers' usual residential address.

Initial shareholdings
Please list the company's subscribers in alphabetical order.

Please use an 'Initial shareholdings' continuation page if necessary.

Subscriber's details	Class of share	Number of shares	Currency	Nominal value of each share	Amount (if any) unpaid	Amount paid
Name MATHEW BROWNING	ORDINARY	20		£1		£20
Address						
Name LEESA BROWNING	ORDINARY	20		£1		£20
Address						
Name SIMON BROWNING	ORDINARY	60		£1		£60
Address						
Name						
Address						
Name						
Address						

Fig. 12. (continued).

IN01
Application to register a company

Part 4   **Statement of guarantee**

Is your company limited by guarantee?
→ **Yes** Complete the sections below.
→ **No** Go to **Part 5** (Statement of compliance).

G1   **Subscribers**

Please complete this section if you are a subscriber of a company limited by guarantee. The following statement is being made by each and every person named below.

I confirm that if the company is wound up while I am a member, or within one year after I cease to be a member, I will contribute to the assets of the company by such amount as may be required for:
- payment of debts and liabilities of the company contracted before I cease to be a member;
- payment of costs, charges and expenses of winding up, and;
- adjustment of the rights of the contributors among ourselves, not exceeding the specified amount below.

❶ Name
Please use capital letters.

❷ Address
The addresses in this section will appear on the public record. They do not have to be the subscribers' usual residential address.

❸ Amount guaranteed
Any valid currency is permitted.

Continuation pages
Please use a 'Subscribers' continuation page if necessary.

Subscriber's details

Forename(s) ❶	
Surname ❶	
Address ❷	
Postcode	
Amount guaranteed ❸	

Subscriber's details

Forename(s) ❶	
Surname ❶	
Address ❷	
Postcode	
Amount guaranteed ❸	

Subscriber's details

Forename(s) ❶	
Surname ❶	
Address ❷	
Postcode	
Amount guaranteed ❸	

Fig. 12. (continued).

IN01

Application to register a company

Subscriber's details	
Forename(s) ❶	
Surname ❶	
Address ❷	
Postcode	
Amount guaranteed ❸	

Subscriber's details	
Forename(s) ❶	
Surname ❶	
Address ❷	
Postcode	
Amount guaranteed ❸	

Subscriber's details	
Forename(s) ❶	
Surname ❶	
Address ❷	
Postcode	
Amount guaranteed ❸	

Subscriber's details	
Forename(s) ❶	
Surname ❶	
Address ❷	
Postcode	
Amount guaranteed ❸	

Subscriber's details	
Forename(s) ❶	
Surname ❶	
Address ❷	
Postcode	
Amount guaranteed ❸	

❶ **Name**
Please use capital letters.

❷ **Address**
The addresses in this section will appear on the public record. They do not have to be the subscribers' usual residential address.

❸ **Amount guaranteed**
Any valid currency is permitted.

Continuation pages
Please use a 'Subscribers' continuation page if necessary.

CHFP000
04/11 Version 4.1

Fig. 12. (continued).

IN01
Application to register a company

Part 5   Statement of compliance

This section must be completed by all companies.

Is the application by an agent on behalf of all the subscribers?

→ **No**   Go to **Section H1** (Statement of compliance delivered by the subscribers).
→ **Yes**   Go to **Section H2** (Statement of compliance delivered by an agent).

H1   Statement of compliance delivered by the subscribers ❶

Please complete this section if the application is not delivered by an agent for the subscribers of the memorandum of association.

I confirm that the requirements of the Companies Act 2006 as to registration have been complied with.

❶ **Statement of compliance delivered by the subscribers** Every subscriber to the memorandum of association must sign the statement of compliance.

Subscriber's signature	Signature X X
Subscriber's signature	Signature X X
Subscriber's signature	Signature X X
Subscriber's signature	Signature X X
Subscriber's signature	Signature X X
Subscriber's signature	Signature X X
Subscriber's signature	Signature X X
Subscriber's signature	Signature X X

Fig. 12. (continued).

IN01
Application to register a company

Subscriber's signature	_Signature_ **X**	**X**
Subscriber's signature	Signature **X**	**X**
Subscriber's signature	Signature **X**	**X**
Subscriber's signature	Signature **X**	**X**

Continuation pages
Please use a 'Statement of compliance delivered by the subscribers' continuation page if more subscribers need to sign.

H2 Statement of compliance delivered by an agent

Please complete this section if this application is delivered by an agent for the subscribers to the memorandum of association.

Agent's name	ROBERT BROWNING
Building name/number	27
Street	CLOCK PARADE
Post town	WARE
County/Region	HERTS
Postcode	S G 1 3 Z Z
Country	ENGLAND

I confirm that the requirements of the Companies Act 2006 as to registration have been complied with.

Agent's signature	Signature **X** **X**

CHFP000
04/11 Version 4.1

Fig. 12. (continued).

IN01
Application to register a company

✓ Certificate

We will send your certificate to the presenters address (shown above) or if indicated to another address shown below:

☐ At the registered office address (Given in Section A6).
☐ At the agents address (Given in Section H2).

✓ Checklist

We may return forms completed incorrectly or with information missing.

Please make sure you have remembered the following:

☐ You have checked that the proposed company name is available as well as the various rules that may affect your choice of name. More information can be found in guidance on our website.
☐ If the name of the company is the same as one already on the register as permitted by The Company and Business Names (Miscellaneous Provisions) Regulations 2008, please attach consent.
☐ You have used the correct appointment sections.
☐ Any addresses given must be a physical location. They cannot be a PO Box number (unless part of a full service address), DX or LP (Legal Post in Scotland) number.
☐ The document has been signed, where indicated.
☐ All relevant attachments have been included.
☐ You have enclosed the Memorandum of Association.
☐ You have enclosed the correct fee.

❗ Important information

Please note that all information on this form will appear on the public record, apart from information relating to usual residential addresses.

£ How to pay

A fee is payable on this form.
Make cheques or postal orders payable to 'Companies House'. For information on fees, go to: www.companieshouse.gov.uk

✉ Where to send

You may return this form to any Companies House address, however for expediency we advise you to return it to the appropriate address below:

For companies registered in England and Wales:
The Registrar of Companies, Companies House, Crown Way, Cardiff, Wales, CF14 3UZ.
DX 33050 Cardiff.

For companies registered in Scotland:
The Registrar of Companies, Companies House, Fourth floor, Edinburgh Quay 2, 139 Fountainbridge, Edinburgh, Scotland, EH3 9FF.
DX ED235 Edinburgh 1
or LP - 4 Edinburgh 2 (Legal Post).

For companies registered in Northern Ireland:
The Registrar of Companies, Companies House, Second Floor, The Linenhall, 32-38 Linenhall Street, Belfast, Northern Ireland, BT2 8BG.
DX 481 N.R. Belfast 1.

Section 243 exemption
If you are applying for, or have been granted a section 243 exemption, please post this whole form to the different postal address below:
The Registrar of Companies, PO Box 4082, Cardiff, CF14 3WE.

ℹ Further information

For further information, please see the guidance notes on the website at www.companieshouse.gov.uk or email enquiries@companieshouse.gov.uk

This form is available in an alternative format. Please visit the forms page on the website at www.companieshouse.gov.uk

This form has been provided free of charge by Companies House.

CHFP000
04/11 Version 4.1

Fig. 12. (continued).

5

Being a Shareholder

Now that your company is set up there are various aspects of being a shareholder to consider. This chapter deals with the more important of those aspects and in particular:

■ paying yourself

■ using your voting power

■ exercising your rights

■ paying dividends

■ limiting your liability.

PAYING YOURSELF

One of the first things that anyone starting a company wants to know is how do they get payment out of the business for their own labours.

If you are a sole trader or are in partnership you can in theory just take the money when you want to. This is commonly known as **drawings** as you are drawing out money on account of profits that you hope will be made. The tax on these 'earnings' is paid later when the profit figures are known.

In a company things are different. As the company is a separate entity it has to pay you either:

■ as an employee by means of a wage, a salary or by commission, or

■ as a shareholder by way of dividend.

Let us consider the implications of each of these in turn.

Payment by wage, salary or commission

A company is required to pay all employees, and that includes directors and the company secretary, assuming they are paid at all, under the PAYE system so that tax is deducted directly at the time of payment. Paying your taxes is discussed further in Chapter 11 but suffice to say if you intend to pay yourself from your company you will have to do it in accordance with the rules that apply to all employees.

You will therefore have to decide how much money your company can afford to pay you and treat that as a wage or salary on a regular basis. Subsequently, you may find that you are taking too much, which either starves the company of cash resources needed for the business or means that the company is just not making enough profit. You will then have to waive your salary for a while till business picks up. What you must not do, in these circumstances, is just draw money out as you would as a sole trader or partnership. The reason for this is simple. The company is a separate entity so if you just draw money out the company is, in effect, lending you money.

> ### NOTE WELL
>
> **Companies are not allowed by law to lend
> money to directors.**

and

> ### EQUALLY
>
> **It is unlawful for companies to pay directors any
> remuneration 'free of tax'.**

This may seem harsh because there is a tendency to think of the money in your company as your own but it is not. It belongs to the company. And the company, like people, has to pay its tax. It is known as corporation tax and the rate is fixed each year by the government in the Budget proposals. For small companies it is normally a similar rate to the standard rate of income tax. Companies are now required to assess their own profits on a similar system to the rules applying to income tax.

Payment by dividend

The profits of a company can be distributed to the shareholders by way of dividend. This means the company decides to pay out so much per share and all shareholders will participate. This may prove difficult if all you are trying to do is pay yourself.

Example

Your company pays a dividend to its shareholders on 31 December. There are 1,000 shares in issue and you and your directors declare a dividend of £2 per share. The company will pay corporation tax on the profits and your shareholders will receive, in respect of each share they hold, £2. The cost to the company is greater by the amount of the tax paid but shareholders will get a tax credit for each share in respect of the corporation tax paid, meaning that the tax is already paid on this income when they receive it, and no more tax at the basic rate is payable by them. They could, however, pay income tax at a higher rate if their overall income is high enough.

There is more information on corporation tax in Chapter 11.

Fringe benefits

There is a further way of paying yourself in a company which should be mentioned. **Fringe benefits** are where the company pays money on your behalf for certain services. The most common fringe benefit is the provision of a company car. The amount upon which tax is payable is a percentage of the list price of the car inclusive of accessories, delivery charges and VAT, but the percentage is reduced depending on the age of the car and the business miles covered. Also note that companies have to pay National Insurance on the taxable value of an employee's company car. If fuel is provided free then there is an additional change to tax.

Other benefits you might enjoy include meals in a canteen provided all employees are entitled to them or the cost of an insurance premium which would pay you if you were unable to work.

Additionally, **benefits** are treated just as if you had earned the money and you are taxed at the rate applicable to your salary plus your benefits less anything you contribute to them. However, this applies only if that figure is £8,500 or more or if you are a director.

Minimising your tax bill

The way you pay yourself is crucial when you are trying to minimise your tax bill. Ideally, you will pay yourself the amount at which the tax rate is equal or lower than the tax rate on the company's profits. Anything above that will attract the higher rate of income tax and that is higher than the small companies corporation tax rate.

The decision of what to pay yourself is complicated and you would do well to take advice from your accountant before you start. However, in the end you will pay yourself what you need for your standard of living or what the company can afford. And you will personally have to bear the tax on that figure.

USING YOUR VOTING POWER

You saw in Chapter 3 that votes are taken, where necessary, at formal meetings of the company and each shareholder has a vote for each share owned. If, therefore, you hold a majority of the shares you will get a majority of the votes and this will enable you to carry out any changes or policy decisions you wish to.

If, however, you only hold 40 per cent of the shares there is potentially 60 per cent of shareholders against you. It is rare in small companies to have such disagreements and probable that, if it were the case, the problem is fundamental and another course of action will be required to resolve it.

In most small companies the only formal decisions to take are at the annual general meeting and those normally involve:

- receiving the report of the directors

- adoption of the accounts for the previous financial year

- re-election of certain directors if the articles require them to stand down

- election or re-election of the auditor (if the company has one).

You would be well advised to think carefully how your shares are distributed amongst the shareholders, as most decisions are put to a normal majority vote.

EXERCISING YOUR RIGHTS

You will not normally be required to exercise most of your rights as a shareholder in a small company. These are put in place by the various Companies Acts and by the provisions of the Memorandum and Articles to deal with intractable problems you may encounter as a shareholder. Should you be involved in a difficult area of company law you must seek advice from a lawyer or accountant as there are precedents (i.e. similar cases that have happened before) for a number of things which can occur.

Knowing what your rights are

There are certain rights that you will exercise on a regular basis. As a shareholder you are entitled to:

- receive proper notice of any meeting of the company, together with copies of any proposed resolutions so that you can attend and vote on them

- receive the financial accounts of the company for the preceding year

- transfer your shares to someone else by agreeing the price with the directors; it is often usual, according to the Articles, for these shares to be offered to the remaining shareholders in the same proportion that they hold their existing shares so that their voting rights do not alter

- call an extraordinary general meeting of the company

- be involved in any reconstruction of the way the company is financed, the sale of the company or its amalgamation with another company

- concur in the modification or variation of any rights, privileges or liabilities attached to the shares.

It is to be hoped that your company will be well run and any difficulties cleared up before you need to exercise your rights. But there must be provision for the unexpected or unforeseen.

PAYING DIVIDENDS

Earlier in this chapter we saw how shareholders could be paid by dividend and the consequent tax implications. Directors recommend dividends. This is done by taking into account the financial position of the company at the time.

Types of dividend

There are two types of **dividend**:

- interim

- final.

Interim dividends can be declared by the directors at any time and a meeting of shareholders is not required to sanction this. The final dividend is agreed by the shareholders at a general meeting when they will also formally agree any interim dividend previously paid. In the absence of any provision to the contrary in the Articles, dividends must always be paid in cash. They must also be paid out of profits.

An equal amount is paid for each share owned but in some companies there can be different classes of shares.

Example
A company is set up with two classes of shares:

1. preference shares

2. ordinary shares.

Preference shares are entitled to a dividend before ordinary shares are. It is usually at a fixed rate and is payable whether the company is doing well or not. Holders of preference shares have put money into the company as a fairly safe investment with a small return of interest. Ordinary shares are much more linked to the fortunes of the company and dividends can vary a lot. Sometimes no dividends are paid at all.

It is probably fair to say that in the majority of small companies payment of dividends is rare as profits are invariably taken as director's salary or other fringe benefits.

LIMITING YOUR LIABILITY

Small companies are in the main set up for one reason, and one reason alone, and that is to limit the financial liability of the shareholders to the amount of the nominal value of the shares they have purchased.

With no limited liability all of a person's assets, including his house, are available to his creditors (the people he owes money to). A limited company, which is a separate legal entity from its individual shareholders and directors, has its own assets and liabilities. But these are nothing to do with the directors or the shareholders personally and hence their liability for the company's financial debts and responsibilities is limited. Unless, of course, the directors have been trading fraudulently.

That all seems fine. But beware.

Other businesses have become aware that unscrupulous businesspeople have taken advantage of this limited liability and run off with company money or assets. Also when you are embarking on a new business venture you have to build up your credibility before you are fully trusted. Therefore you may be asked for personal guarantees against your business debts. Note that:

- banks, in particular, will ask for guarantees for an overdraft facility or a loan

- this can also apply to leasing agreements

- landlords may also consider this in respect of rent

- even normal suppliers may insist on it for normal credit arrangements.

Once any of them do this your limited liability is severely impaired. Do not think that limited liability removes all your business worries. It can sometimes make them more of a headache.

ACTION POINTS AND REMINDERS

1. Decide how much to pay yourself but don't overdo it.

2. How will you pay your tax? It is due each month.

3. See your accountant about paying dividends and make sure it is necessary.

4. If you are having a company-owned car you must keep adequate and accurate records of the expense.

5. Make sure you own the majority of the shares.

6. You may have to give someone dealing with your company a personal guarantee so be prepared.

6

Being a Director

Your company is now set up. Your registered office is fixed, your directors and secretary are in place, your shareholders have paid in their money and the rest of the formalities are complete.

You must now carefully check through your responsibilities as a director. This chapter looks at those responsibilities in more depth and includes:

- fulfilling your responsibilities

- wrongful trading

- completing your Annual Return

- filing your accounts.

FULFILLING YOUR RESPONSIBILITIES

Directors, as guardians of their companies, are appointed to manage the affairs of a company. This includes keeping the affairs of the company within the law, and there are some legal requirements of the Companies Act which must be carried out.

Every director has a personal responsibility to see that certain documents are delivered to the Registrar of Companies. They include:

- the company's annual accounts

- the Annual Return

- notification of any change of directors or their particulars

- notification of any change of secretary or their particulars

- notification of a change of registered office

- notification of any mortgages or charges levied on the company

- notification of any changes in the Memorandum or Articles of Association

- notification of the company going into liquidation or receivership.

If you fail to send in your accounts on time a rising scale of fines is imposed on a private company if the documents are over 12 months late. It only applies to accounts and is known as a late filing penalty. It is payable by the company. Note that there can also be fines levied on a director personally for not delivering accounts, but this would only be as a result of his prosecution for the offence and would be set by the court.

Failure to submit the other documents can also result in fines on the director personally.

How do you avoid fines and penalties?
Simple.

Ensure that your accounts, your annual return and any other documents are submitted well on time.

Documents have to be sent to:

The Registrar of Companies
Crown Way
Cardiff CF14 3UZ

for companies in England and Wales. There are other offices if you prefer to deliver them by hand and these are in London, Manchester, Birmingham and Leeds.

For companies in Scotland documents should be sent to:

The Registrar of Companies
Companies House
4th Floor Edinburgh Quay 2
139 Fountainbridge
Edinburgh EH3 9FF

There is also an office in Glasgow for hand deliveries.

For companies in Northern Ireland the address is:

The Registrar of Companies
Companies House
Second Floor
The Linenhall
32–38 Linenhall Street
Belfast
Northern Ireland
BT2 8BG

It is now possible to file nearly all the documents required by the Registrar of Companies online. Be certain to obtain an acknowledgement of their receipt. Do not incur a penalty by not filing properly.

A number of companies delegate the responsibilities for sending in documents to their accountants or financial advisers as they usually prepare the accounts and are in possession of other relevant information. Again, beware. It is your job as a director to make sure the job is being done.

It is not your accountants or financial advisers who face prosecution or penalties.

It is YOU.

Finally, all this statutory information is needed to make it available for public inspection. This enables other individuals or businesses to form a view of a company with which they may wish to deal. It is also part of the protection which is necessary if companies are going to have the benefit of limited liability.

WRONGFUL TRADING

As a director you ought to know if your company is insolvent, i.e. has no assets with which to pay debts owed by the company. If it is, you are duty bound to declare the company insolvent and go into **liquidation**, which is the process used to wind up the business of a company.

You also have a duty to the creditors of your company (i.e. businesses or individuals the company owes money to) not to continue trading when there is no reasonable prospect of avoiding liquidation.

If the company goes into insolvent liquidation, the liquidator may apply to the court if he can prove that you knew, or ought to have known, prior to the liquidation that the company could not avoid taking that course. This is known as **wrongful trading**.

In these circumstances the court would make you personally liable to contribute to the company's assets and disqualify you from being a director again for up to 15 years. You will not be liable, however, if you can show that you have taken every step, prior to liquidation, to minimise the potential loss to the company's creditors.

Further, if you knowingly intended to defraud your creditors it is **fraudulent trading**. You may still be expected to contribute to the assets of the company but may additionally be fined or even imprisoned.

> **It is your job as a director to see that your company can pay its debts and therefore avoid being accused of wrongful trading.**

COMPLETING YOUR ANNUAL RETURN

It is the directors' responsibility to see that the Annual Return (Form AR01, see Figure 13) is sent to the Registrar on time. It is now customary for the Registrar to ask you to complete this form online but your company must be registered for PROOF, a web filing system.

The Annual Return contains the following information:

■ the company number

■ the company name

■ the type of company (e.g. private company limited by shares)

■ the date up to which the return is to be made

■ the address of the registered office

■ the trade classification (identifying the principal activity by a code number)

■ the address where the Register of members is kept

■ the name and address of the company secretary

■ a list of the directors showing, in each case, their name, address, date of birth, nationality and occupation

■ details of the shares issued showing the class, the number and the nominal value

■ a list of the members (i.e. shareholders) which contains names, addresses, number of shares held and dates of transfers if any.

The form, which can be signed and dated by a director or the secretary, is then sent, together with a cheque for £30 filing fee, to the appropriate Registrar.

AR01
Annual Return

This form is part of the PROOF scheme. If your company is registered for PROOF, paper versions of this form will be rejected and sent back to the registered address. Avoid unnecessary rejection and file online. You can view you company's PROOF status on the WebFiling Menu Screen.

Companies House

A fee is payable with this form	You can use the WebFiling service to file this form online.
Please see 'How to pay' on the last page.	Please go to www.companieshouse.gov.uk

✓ **What this form is for**	✗ **What this form is NOT for**	For further information, please
You may use this form to confirm that the company information is correct as at the date of this return. You must file an Annual Return at least once every year.	You cannot use this form to give notice of changes to the company officers, registered office address, company type or information relating to the company records.	refer to our guidance at www.companieshouse.gov.uk

Part 1   Company details

The section must be completed by all companies.

→ **Filling in this form**
Please complete in typescript or in bold black capitals.

All fields are mandatory unless specified or indicated by *

A1   Company details

Company number: 2 9 5 8 1 4 1

Company name in full ❶: SINCLAIR BROOK LTD

❶ **Company name change**
If your company has recently changed its name, please provide the company name as at the date of this return.

A2   Return date

Please give the annual return made up date. The return date must not be a future date. The annual return must be delivered within 28 days of the date given below.

Date of this return ❷: 3 1 / 1 2 / 2 0 X X

❷ **Date of this return**
Your company's return date is usually the anniversary of incorporation or the anniversary of the last annual return filed at Companies House. You may choose an earlier return date but it must not be a later date.

A3   Principal business activity

Please show the trade classification code number(s) for the principal activity or activities. ❸

Classification code 1: 9 3 0 3
Classification code 2:
Classification code 3:
Classification code 4:

If you cannot determine a code, please give a brief description of your business activity below:

Principal activity description:

❸ **Principal business activity**
You must provide a trade classification code (SIC code) or a description of your company's main business in this section.

A full list of the trade classification codes are available on our website: www.companieshouse.gov.uk

CHFP000
10/11 Version 4.2

Fig. 13. Annual Return (Form AR01).

AR01
Annual Return

A4   Company type ❶

Please confirm your company type by ticking the appropriate box below (only one box must be ticked):

- ☐ Public limited company
- ☑ Private company limited by shares
- ☐ Private company limited by guarantee
- ☐ Private company limited by shares exempt under section 60
- ☐ Private company limited by guarantee exempt under section 60
- ☐ Private unlimited company with share capital
- ☐ Private unlimited company without share capital

❶ **Company type**
If you are unsure of your company type, please check your latest certificate of incorporation or our website:
www.companieshouse.gov.uk

A5   Registered office address ❷

Building name/number	PELICAN HOUSE
Street	HIGH STREET
Post town	WARE
County/Region	HERTS
Postcode	S G 1 2 4 Z K

❷ **Change of registered office**
This must agree with the address that is held on the Companies House record at the date of this return.

If the registered office address has changed, you should complete form **AD01** and submit it together with this annual return.

A6   Single alternative inspection location (SAIL) of the company records (if applicable) ❸

Building name/number	
Street	
Post town	
County/Region	
Postcode	

❸ **SAIL address**
This must agree with the address that is held on the Companies House record at the date of this return.

If the address has changed, you should complete form **AD02** and submit it together with this annual return.

A7   Location of company records ❹

Please tick the appropriate box to indicate which records are kept at the SAIL address in **Section A6**:

- ☑ Register of members.
- ☑ Register of directors.
- ☐ Directors' service contracts.
- ☐ Directors' indemnities.
- ☑ Register of secretaries.
- ☑ Records of resolutions etc.
- ☐ Contracts relating to purchase of own shares.
- ☐ Documents relating to redemption or purchase of own share out of capital by private company.
- ☐ Register of debenture holders.
- ☐ Report to members of outcome of investigation by public company into interests in its shares.
- ☐ Register of interests in shares disclosed to public company.
- ☐ Instruments creating charges and register of charges: England and Wales or Northern Ireland.
- ☐ Instruments creating charges and register of charges: Scotland.

❹ **Location of company records**
If the company records are held at the registered office address, **do not** tick any of the boxes in this section.

Certain records must be kept by every company while other records are only kept by certain company types where appropriate.

If the records are not kept at the SAIL address, they must be available at the registered office.

If any of the company records have moved from the registered office to the address in Section A6 since the last annual return, you must complete form **AD03** and submit it together with this annual return.

CHFP000
10/11 Version 4.2

Fig. 13. (continued).

AR01
Annual Return

Part 2 — Officers of the company

This section should include details of the company at the date to which this annual return is made up.

→ For a **secretary** who is an individual, go to **Section B1**.
→ For a **corporate secretary**, go to **Section C1**.
→ For a **director** who is an individual, go to **Section D1**.
→ For a **corporate director**, go to **Section E1**.

Continuation pages
Please use a continuation page if you need to enter more officer details.

Secretary

B1 — **Secretary's details** ❶

Please use this section to list all the secretaries of the company.
For a corporate secretary, complete Section C1-C4.

Title*	MRS
Full forename(s)	LEESA
Surname	BROWNING
Former name(s) ❷	

❶ **Secretary appointments**
You may not use this form to appoint a secretary. To do this, please complete form **AP03** and submit it together with this annual return.

Corporate details
Please use **Section C1-C4** to enter corporate secretary details.

Secretary details
All details must agree with those previously notified to Companies House. If you have made changes since the last annual return and have not notified us, please complete form **CH03**.

❷ **Former name(s)**
Please provide any previous names which have been used for business purposes during the period of this return. Married women do not need to give former names unless previously used for business purposes.

B2 — **Secretary's service address** ❸

Building name/number	21
Street	COLE GREEN ROAD
Post town	HERTFORD
County/Region	HERTS
Postcode	S G 1 4 0 X X
Country	

❸ **Service address**
If you have previously notified Companies House that the service address is at 'The Company's Registered Office', please state 'The Company's Registered Office' in the address.

This information will appear on the public record.

CHFP000
10/11 Version 4.2

Fig. 13. (continued).

AR01
Annual Return

Corporate secretary

C1 Corporate secretary's details ❶

Please use this section to list all the corporate secretaries of the company.

Corporate body/firm name	
Building name/number	
Street	
Post town	
County/Region	
Postcode	
Country	

❶ Corporate secretary appointments
You cannot use this form to appoint a corporate secretary. To do this, please complete form **AP04** and submit it together with this annual return.

Corporate secretary details
All details must agree with those previously notified to Companies House. If you have made changes since the last annual return and have not notified us, please complete form **CH04**.

This information will appear on the public record.

C2 Location of the registry of the corporate body or firm

Is the corporate secretary registered within the European Economic Area (EEA)?
→ **Yes** Complete **Section C3 only**
→ **No** Complete **Section C4 only**

C3 EEA companies ❷

Please give details of the register where the company file is kept (including the relevant state) and the registration number in that register.

Where the company/firm is registered ❸	
Registration number	

❷ EEA
A full list of countries of the EEA can be found in our guidance:
www.companieshouse.gov.uk

❸ This is the register mentioned in Article 3 of the First Company Law Directive (68/151/EEC).

C4 Non-EEA companies

Please give details of the legal form of the corporate body or firm and the law by which it is governed. If applicable, please also give details of the register in which it is entered (including the state) and its registration number in that register.

Legal form of the corporate body or firm	
Governing law	
If applicable, where the company/firm is registered ❹	
If applicable, the registration number	

❹ Non-EEA
Where you have provided details of the register (including state) where the company or firm is registered, you must also provide its number in that register.

CHFP000
10/11 Version 4.2

Fig. 13. (continued).

AR01
Annual Return

Director

D1   **Director's details** ❶

Please use this section to list all the directors of the company.
For a corporate director, complete Section E1-E4.

Title*	MR
Full forename(s)	MATTHEW
Surname	BROWNING
Former name(s) ❷	
Country/State of residence	ENGLAND
Nationality	BRITISH
Date of birth	0 8 0 7 1 9 6 4
Business occupation (if any)	

❶ **Director appointments**
You cannot use this form to appoint a director. To do this, please complete form **AP01** and submit it together with this annual return.

Corporate details
Please use **Section E1-E4** to enter corporate director details.

Director details
All details must agree with those previously notified to Companies House. If you have made changes since the last annual return and have not notified us, please complete form **CH01**.

❷ **Former name(s)**
Please provide any previous names which have been used for business purposes during the period of this return. Married women do not need to give former names unless previously used for business purposes.

D2   **Director's service address** ❸

Building name/number	27
Street	HAILEYBURY STREET
Post town	MELBOURN
County/Region	HERTS
Postcode	S G 1 7 0 X X
Country	ENGLAND

❸ **Service address**
If you have previously notified Companies House that the service address is at 'The Company's Registered Office', please state 'The Company's Registered Office' in the address.

This information will appear on the public record.

Fig. 13. (continued).

AR01
Annual Return

Director

D1 **Director's details** ❶

	Please use this section to list all the directors of the company. **For a corporate director, complete Section E1-E4.**
Title*	MR
Full forename(s)	SIMON
Surname	BROWNING
Former name(s) ❷	
Country/State of residence	
Nationality	
Date of birth	0 1 1 2 1 9 6 2
Business occupation (if any)	

❶ **Director appointments**
You cannot use this form to appoint a director. To do this, please complete form **AP01** and submit it together with this annual return.

Corporate details
Please use **Section E1-E4** to enter corporate director details.

Director details
All details must agree with those previously notified to Companies House. If you have made changes since the last annual return and have not notified us, please complete form **CH01**.

❷ **Former name(s)**
Please provide any previous names which have been used for business purposes during the period of this return. Married women do not need to give former names unless previously used for business purposes.

D2 **Director's service address** ❸

Building name/number	62
Street	FARMERS ROAD
Post town	BRAUGHING
County/Region	HERTS
Postcode	S G 1 7 0 X X
Country	ENGLAND

❸ **Service address**
If you have previously notified Companies House that the service address is at 'The Company's Registered Office', please state 'The Company's Registered Office' in the address.

This information will appear on the public record.

Fig. 13. (continued).

AR01
Annual Return

Corporate director

E1 Corporate director's details ❶

Please use this section to list all the corporate director's of the company.

Corporate body/firm name	
Building name/number	
Street	
Post town	
County/Region	
Postcode	
Country	

❶ **Corporate director appointments**
You cannot use this form to appoint a corporate director. To do this, please complete form **AP02** and submit it together with this annual return.

Corporate director details
All details must agree with those previously notified to Companies House. If you have made changes since the last annual return and have not notified us, please complete form **CH02**.

This information will appear on the public record.

E2 Location of the registry of the corporate body or firm

Is the corporate director registered within the European Economic Area (EEA)?
→ **Yes** Complete **Section E3 only**
→ **No** Complete **Section E4 only**

E3 EEA companies ❷

Please give details of the register where the company file is kept (including the relevant state) and the registration number in that register.

Where the company/firm is registered ❸	
Registration number	

❷ **EEA**
A full list of countries of the EEA can be found in our guidance:
www.companieshouse.gov.uk

❸ This is the register mentioned in Article 3 of the First Company Law Directive (68/151/EEC).

E4 Non-EEA companies

Please give details of the legal form of the corporate body or firm and the law by which it is governed. If applicable, please also give details of the register in which it is entered (including the state) and its registration number in that register.

Legal form of the corporate body or firm	
Governing law	
If applicable, where the company/firm is registered ❹	
If applicable, the registration number	

❹ **Non-EEA**
Where you have provided details of the register (including state) where the company or firm is registered, you must also provide its number in that register

CHFP000
10/11 Version 4.2

Fig. 13. (continued).

AR01
Annual Return

Part 3	**Statement of capital ❶**

Does your company have share capital?
→ **Yes** Complete the sections below and the following **Part 4**.
→ **No** Go to **Part 5 (Signature)**.

❶ This should reflect the company's capital status at the made up date of this annual return.

F1   Share capital in pound sterling (£)

Please complete the table below to show each class of shares held in pound sterling.
If all your issued capital is in sterling, only complete **Section F1** and then go to **Section F4**.

Class of shares (E.g. Ordinary/Preference etc.)	Amount paid up on each share ❷	Amount (if any) unpaid on each share ❷	Number of shares ❸	Aggregate nominal value ❹
ORDINARY	£1		1000	£ 1000
				£
				£
				£
		Totals		£

F2   Share capital in other currencies

Please complete the table below to show any class of shares held in other currencies.
Please complete a separate table for each currency.

Currency

Class of shares (E.g. Ordinary/Preference etc.)	Amount paid up on each share ❷	Amount (if any) unpaid on each share ❷	Number of shares ❸	Aggregate nominal value ❹
		Totals		

Currency

Class of shares (E.g. Ordinary/Preference etc.)	Amount paid up on each share ❷	Amount (if any) unpaid on each share ❷	Number of shares ❸	Aggregate nominal value ❹
		Totals		

F3   Totals

Please give the total number of shares and total aggregate nominal value of issued share capital.

❺ **Total aggregate nominal value**
Please list total aggregate values in different currencies separately. For example: £100 + €100 + $10 etc.

Total number of shares	1000
Total aggregate nominal value ❺	£1000

❷ Including both the nominal value and any share premium.
❸ Total number of issued shares in this class.
❹ Number of shares issued multiplied by nominal value of each share.

Continuation Pages
Please use a Statement of Capital continuation page if necessary.

CHFP000
10/11 Version 4.2

Fig. 13. (continued).

AR01
Annual Return

F4	**Statement of capital** (Voting rights)

Please give the prescribed particulars of rights attached to shares for each class of share shown in the statement of capital share tables in **Sections F1** and **F2**.

Class of share

Voting rights

Class of share

Voting rights

Class of share

Voting rights

Class of share

Voting rights

Fig. 13. (continued).

Part 4	**Shareholders**	
	Does your company have share capital?	❶ This should reflect the shareholder details at the made up date of this annual return.
	→ **Yes** Complete the sections below.	
	→ **No** Go to **Part 5 (Signature).**	

G1	**Traded public companies ❷**	
	☐ Please tick the box if your company was a traded public company at any time during the period of this return.	❷ **Traded company definition** A traded company means a company any of whose shares are admitted to trading on a regulated market.

G2	**List of past and present shareholders**

Private and non-traded public companies are required to provide a 'full list' if one was not included with either of the last two returns.

Traded public companies are required to provide a list of shareholders who held at least 5% of the issued shares of any share class if a list was not provided with either of the last two returns.

Please tick the appropriate box below:

☐ A full list of shareholders for a private or non-traded public company is enclosed. Please complete **Section G3**; or

☐ A list of shareholders holding at least 5% of the issued shares of any share class for a traded public company is enclosed. Please complete **Section G4**.

☐ A list of shareholder changes is enclosed.
→ For private or non-traded public companies, please complete **Section G3**.
→ For traded public companies, please complete **Section G4**.

☐ There were no shareholder changes in this period.
→ Go to **Part 5 (Signature).**

Please tick the appropriate box below to indicate the format of your shareholder details:
☐ The list of shareholders is enclosed on paper.
☐ The list of shareholders is enclosed in another format.

Fig. 13. (continued).

AR01
Annual Return

Private or non-traded public companies – list of past and present shareholders

This section should only be completed by companies that have not traded on a regulated market at any time during the period of this return.

Changes during this period to shareholders' particulars or details of the amount of stock or shares transferred must be completed each year.

You must provide a 'full list' of all company shareholders on:
- The company's first annual return following incorporation;
- Every third annual return after a full list has been provided.

Please list the company shareholders in alphabetical order.

Joint shareholders should be listed consecutively.

Further shareholders
Please use a 'Private or non-traded public companies – list of past and present shareholders' continuation page if necessary.

Shareholder's Name (Address not required)	Class of share	Shares or stock currently held — Number of shares or amount of stock	Shares or stock transferred (if appropriate) — Number of shares or amount of stock	Date of registration of transfer
MATTHEW BROWNING	ORDINARY	200		/ /
LEESA BROWNING	ORDINARY	200		/ /
SIMON BROWNING	ORDINARY	600		/ /
				/ /
				/ /
				/ /
				/ /
				/ /
				/ /
				/ /
				/ /
				/ /
				/ /
				/ /

CHFP000
10/11 Version 4.2

Fig. 13. (continued).

AR01
Annual Return

Traded public companies – list of past and present shareholders

This section should show the shareholders that hold at **least 5%** of any class of share(s) of the company at the date of this return. It should only be completed by public companies that have traded on a regulated market at any time during the period of this return.

Changes during this period to shareholders' particulars or details of the amount of stock or shares transferred must be completed each year.

You must provide a 'full list' of all company shareholders on:
- The company's first annual return following incorporation;
- Every third annual return after a full list has been provided.

Please list the company shareholders in alphabetical order.

Joint shareholders should be listed consecutively.

Further shareholders
Please use a 'Traded public companies – list of past and present shareholders' continuation page if necessary.

Shareholder's details	Class of share	Shares or stock currently held — Number of shares or amount of stock	Shares or stock transferred (if appropriate) Number of shares or amount of stock	Date of registration of transfer
Name				/ /
Address				/ /
				/ /
Name				/ /
Address				/ /
				/ /
Name				/ /
Address				/ /
				/ /
Name				/ /
Address				/ /
				/ /

Fig. 13. (continued).

AR01
Annual Return

Part 5 — Signature

This must be completed by all companies.

I am signing this form on behalf of the company.

Signature

Signature

X   X

This form may be signed by:
Director ❶, Secretary, Person authorised ❷, Charity commission receiver and
manager, CIC manager, Judicial factor.

❶ **Societas Europaea**
If the form is being filed on behalf
of a Societas Europaea (SE) please
delete 'director' and insert details
of which organ of the SE the person
signing has membership.

❷ **Person authorised**
Under either section 270 or 274 of
the Companies Act 2006.

Fig. 13. (continued).

AR01
Annual Return

Fig. 13. (continued).

Where the directors' or secretary's details change, you need to complete form CH01. AR01 can only be used to confirm these changes or when that change coincides with the date of the return.

FILING YOUR ACCOUNTS

All companies have to keep accounting records for each financial period, normally a year, and must send their accounts to the Registrar of Companies within nine months of the chosen year end.

Accounting reference date

The first accounts of a company start with the date of incorporation and run to the accounting reference date, which is the date decided by the company and which is the most convenient for their year to end (for example, 31 December). The accounting reference date is chosen by sending to the Registrar form AA01 (see Figure 14). If you fail to choose a date the Registrar will choose one for you. It will be the last day of the month of the anniversary of incorporation.

A company may make up its accounts to a date seven days either side of the accounting reference date, which may be useful, for example, for a retail shop that wishes its year to end on a Saturday. The period ending on the accounting reference date must be more than six months and less than 18 months.

You can change the accounting reference date within limits. This notifies the Registrar that you wish to shorten or extend the current period and will state the new date. But you cannot:

In accordance with
Section 392 of the
Companies Act 2006.

AA01

Change of accounting reference date

Companies House
— for the record —

You can use the WebFiling service to file this form online.
Please go to www.companieshouse.gov.uk

✓ **What this form is for**
You may use this form
to change the accounting reference
date relating to either the current, or
the immediately previous,
accounting period.

✗ **What this form is NOT for**
You cannot use this form to
- change a period for which the
  accounts are already overdue; or
- extend a period beyond 18
  months unless the company is in
  administration.

For further information, please
refer to our guidance at
www.companieshouse.gov.uk

---

1 | **Company details**

Company number	`2` `9` `5` `8` `1` `4` `1`
Company name in full	SINCLAIR BROOK LTD

→ **Filling in this form**
Please complete in typescript or in
bold black capitals.

All fields are mandatory unless
specified or indicated by *

---

2 | **Date of accounting reference period**

Please enter the end date of the current, or the immediately previous,
accounting period. **❶**

Accounting period
ending on | `d 3` `d 1`   `m 1` `m 2`   `y 2` `y 0` `y X` `y X`

❶ Date of period you wish to change
The current period means the
present accounting period which
has not yet come to an end.

The immediately previous period
means the period immediately
preceding your present accounting
period.

---

3 | **New accounting reference date ❷**

Has the accounting reference period been shortened or extended?
→ **Shortened.** Please complete 'Date shortened so as to end on'.
→ **Extended.** Please complete 'Date extended so as to end on'.

Please enter the date the accounting reference period has been shortened to.

Date **Shortened** so as
to end on | `d` `d`   `m` `m`   `y` `y` `y` `y`

or

Please enter the date the accounting reference period has been extended to.

Date **Extended** so as
to end on | `d 3` `d 1`   `m 0` `m 1`   `y 2` `y 0` `y X` `y X`

❷ New accounting reference date
If you wish to move the end of your
current, or immediately previous,
reference period to an earlier date,
please insert the required date in the
box marked 'Shortened'.

If you wish to move the end of your
current, or immediately previous,
reference period to a later date,
please insert the required date in the
box marked 'Extended'.

You cannot change a period for
which the accounts are overdue.

You cannot extend a period beyond
18 months unless the company is in
administration.

BIS | Department for Business
Innovation & Skills

CHFP000
05/10 Version 4.0

Fig. 14. Change of accounting reference date (Form AA01).

AA01
Change of accounting reference date

---

4   **Extending more than once in five years ❶**

Have you extended the accounting reference period more than once in five years? → **Yes.** Please complete the section below. → **No.** Please go to **Section 5.**	❶ **Extending more than once in five years** You only need to complete this section if you have extended your accounting reference period more than once in five years.

Extending more than once in five years

You **may not** extend periods more than once in five years unless you fall into one of the following categories. Please tick only one box.

☐   The company is in administration.

☐   You have specific approval from the Secretary of State (please enclose a copy).

☐   You are extending the company's accounting reference period to align with that of a parent or subsidiary undertaking established in the European Economic Area.

☐   You are submitting the form on behalf of an overseas company.

---

5   **Signature**

I am signing this form on behalf of the company.

Signature

Signature

X   X

This form may be signed by:
Director ❷, Secretary, Person authorised ❸, Permanent representative on behalf of an overseas company, Administrator, Administrative receiver, Receiver, Receiver manager, Charity commission receiver and manager, CIC manager, Judicial factor.

❷ **Societas Europaea**
If the form is being filed on behalf of a Societas Europaea (SE), please delete 'director' and insert details of which organ of the SE the person signing has membership.

❸ **Person authorised**
Under either section 270 or 274 of the Companies Act 2006.

CHFP000
05/10 Version 4.0

Fig. 14. (continued).

AA01
Change of accounting reference date

✔ Checklist

We may return forms completed incorrectly or with information missing.

Please make sure you have remembered the following:
- ☐ The company name and number match the information held on the public Register.
- ☐ You have completed section 2.
- ☐ You have entered the new accounting reference date in section 3.
- ☐ You have completed section 4 (if appropriate).
- ☐ You have signed the form.
- ☐ You have checked your filing deadline through WebCHeck at www.companieshouse.gov.uk

❗ Important information

Please note that all information on this form will appear on the public record.

✉ Where to send

You may return this form to any Companies House address, however for expediency we advise you to return it to the appropriate address below:

For companies registered in England and Wales:
The Registrar of Companies, Companies House, Crown Way, Cardiff, Wales, CF14 3UZ.
DX 33050 Cardiff.

For companies registered in Scotland:
The Registrar of Companies, Companies House, Fourth floor, Edinburgh Quay 2, 139 Fountainbridge, Edinburgh, Scotland, EH3 9FF.
DX ED235 Edinburgh 1
or LP - 4 Edinburgh 2 (Legal Post).

For companies registered in Northern Ireland:
The Registrar of Companies, Companies House, Second Floor, The Linenhall, 32-38 Linenhall Street,, Belfast, Northern Ireland, BT2 8BG.
DX 481 N.R. Belfast 1.

ℹ Further information

For further information, please see the guidance notes on the website at www.companieshouse.gov.uk or email enquiries@companieshouse.gov.uk

This form is available in an alternative format. Please visit the forms page on the website at www.companieshouse.gov.uk

CHFP000
05/10 Version 4.0

Fig. 14. (continued).

- extend it to more than 18 months

- extend it more than once in five years.

Note that when companies own other companies or a company is directed to by the Secretary of State these rules may be altered.

The Registrar will reject your company's accounts if they are made up to a date which is more than seven days before or after the accounting reference date.

The accounts

All limited companies must send their **Directors' Report** and Accounts to the Registrar of Companies. This must be done within nine months of the accounting reference date and a new company must send its first accounts within 21 months of incorporation.

Your accounts have only to be approved by the directors and signed by one of them. They do not have to be laid before a general meeting of the company's shareholders nor do they have to be agreed by HMRC. They should be on white A4 paper with black print.

The Directors' Report must be signed by an officer of the company (director or secretary) and the Auditor's Report must state their name and be signed by them.

The accounts include:

- a **profit and loss account** (or income and expenditure account if the company is not trading for profit)

- a balance sheet

- an Auditor's Report

- a Directors' Report.

Small companies

There are special rules which govern the way a small company deals with its accounts. To be a 'small company' it must meet two of the following three criteria:

1. Its sales must not exceed £5,600,000.

2. Its balance sheet total must not exceed £2,800,000.

3. Its number of employees must not exceed 50.

Small companies may send abbreviated accounts to the Registrar, which consist of an abbreviated **balance sheet** and a special Auditor's Report. Above their signature the directors must make a statement saying that they have relied on the exemptions for individual accounts on the grounds that the company is entitled to the benefit of those exemptions as a small company. The special Auditor's Report should also state that the requirements for exemptions are satisfied.

In these cases a full set of accounts, with a full audit report, must still be provided for the company members.

The audit

Small companies need not necessarily have an audit. The regulations for exemption are set out in Chapter 8. However, an audit can be demanded by a member holding more than ten per cent of the shares.

Where the company is eligible (i.e. it has a balance sheet total of not more than £2,800,000) and audited accounts are not needed, the balance sheet signed by the directors must contain statements that:

1. The directors are of the opinion that the company is entitled to the exemption from audit conferred by section 444(1) of the Companies Act 2006;

2. No notice from members requiring an audit has been deposited under the Companies Act 2006, and

3. The directors acknowledge their responsibilities for:
    (a) ensuring that the company keeps accounting records which comply with the Companies Act 2006, and
    (b) preparing accounts which give a true and fair view of the state of affairs of the company at the end of the financial year, and of its profit and loss for the financial year in accordance with the requirements, and which otherwise comply with the requirements of the Act relating to accounts, so far as applicable to the company.

Although you can see it is possible not to have an audit, it is preferable as accounts are often used by third parties to assess your business. They are comforted by a clean Auditor's Report and the Inspector of Taxes also prefers it. It will cost more however.

A typical Auditor's Report where there is no audit undertaken might say:

'As described on the Balance Sheet you are responsible for the preparation of the accounts for the year ended . . . , set out on pages . . . , and you consider that the company is exempt from an audit and a report under section 444 of the Companies Act 2006. In accordance with your instructions we have compiled these unaudited accounts in order to assist you to fulfil your statutory responsibilities from the accounting records and information and explanations supplied to us.'

You can see what it means to say the directors have the responsibility for the accounts when no audit takes place.

Avoiding penalties

Remember to avoid penalties by:

- submitting forms within the time limit

- ensuring all forms have original signatures and are dated

- presenting forms and accounts in a clear and legible form approved by Companies House.

ACTION POINTS AND REMINDERS

1. You do realise that there are a number of responsibilities that you as a director of a company have and that there are fines for not carrying them out.

2. Certain basic forms must be submitted to the Registrar of Companies each year and you should know what they are.

3. The forms must be sent to the Registrar of Companies.

4. When you hand over the job of completing the forms to your accountant it is still you who is responsible for sending them in.

5. If you cannot pay the people you owe money, consider what you should do.

6. The Registrar makes it easy for you to send in your annual return by completing it with the information he or she has on file. You only have to amend it if necessary.

7. Make sure your accounting reference date is suitable for your needs.

8. Your accounts should be sent in to the Registrar of Companies with the Annual Return.

9. You do not necessarily have to have an audit.

Preparing for Business

Before you embark on any business venture you must prepare the ground. It is important to cultivate an image which will leave a lasting impression on the people you deal with. This chapter sets out the important elements of the preparation necessary for success. They include:

- choosing your name

- opening your bank account

- employing your staff

- equipping your business.

CHOOSING YOUR NAME

If you have already started your business you may well have decided on a name. This may be your own name or one you have given it. It is a good idea to choose the name with care. Your future marketing may be helped or hindered by the name you choose.

For example, let us suppose your name is John Nelson, you live in Brockenhurst and you are starting a business as a printer. You have an infinite number of options for naming your business. Here are a few:

■   John Nelson Printers Ltd

■   J N Printers Ltd

■   Nelson Printers Ltd

■   Brockenhurst Printers Ltd

■   Masterprinters Ltd.

Now consider some advantages and disadvantages of these names.

'John Nelson Printers Ltd' immediately identifies the business with you. This is useful when the people you deal with know you. If they do not know you then 'J N Printers Ltd' is just as good. 'Nelson Printers Ltd' also identifies you and is shorter and easier to remember whereas 'Brockenhurst Printers Ltd' lets people know where the business is situated – unless you later move but cannot find premises in Brockenhurst! 'Masterprinters Ltd' is a description of what you do but does not say who you are or where it is.

Imagine your business expands in the future and you wish to move your works or open another branch in, say, Winchester. The identification with Brockenhurst then becomes a liability as Brockenhurst is no longer the home of the business.

So you see it is worth taking a little time in deciding what your business name is going to be. Remember to check with Companies House that the name you want is available. For full details of requirements you may need to refer to the Business Names Act 1985.

Opening your bank account

It is essential for a business to operate its financial transactions by using a bank account. This has a number of advantages:

- It is a permanent and independent record of your transactions.

- It provides a place to put your money until it is needed.

- It enables you to get rid of excess cash if you are in a cash business.

- It allows you to pay the people you owe money to conveniently and efficiently.

- It enables you to secure a loan or an overdraft when this is necessary.

- It gives you access to a range of other services.

Banks, like any other business, are keen to get more customers. If you are starting a new business there is every chance that most banks will be offering generous terms for you to join them. For example, they may offer free banking for the first 12 months of trading if you remain in credit, that is if you have some money in your account all the time.

Shop around and see what all the banks have to offer before settling on one bank.

Bank managers are human despite what some people may say. They are in business to make a profit just as you are and they want to see a sound business idea before they think of risking their money.

So if you are going to see a bank manager make sure you have done your homework first. He or she is interested in what you are going to do, where you are going to do it and how much money you are going to need to carry it out. These objectives must be clear in your mind.

Questions you should have answers to

- What will happen if your idea doesn't work?

- What will happen if you do not get the sales you expect?

- How much money will you be putting into the business?

- How much do you expect to take out regularly to live on?

Be the master of the facts and give your bank manager the confidence that you really know what you are talking about.

Opening a company bank account

As with most things these days you will have to complete a form. This will probably be in some detail as the bank will be contracting with the company and not you as an individual. They must get all the information they can.

General information required will normally be:

- name of the company

▪ company number

▪ registered address, telephone number, etc.

▪ date of incorporation

▪ date of financial year end

▪ approximate expected **turnover**

▪ names, addresses, and details of directors and secretary

▪ address from which the account will be run (if different from
  the registered address) and where statements should be sent

▪ number of cheque books and paying in books required.

In addition the bank will require a bank mandate (see Figure 15).
This document will specify that on a certain date the directors
held a meeting of the board and decided to appoint a particular
banker. It also decided that the signatories were to be, say, any
two of the directors and the secretary. This mandate would be
signed by the chairman of the meeting. It would also contain
specimen signatures of the people designated to sign on behalf
of the company.

Once these formalities are completed the bank will open the
account for business transactions.

Name of company	SINCLAIR BROOK LTD.
Company's registered number	2958141

At a meeting of the
Board of Directors on

Day Month Year
01   08   0X

It was resolved that
Barclays Bank PLC ('Barclays')

be appointed as our bankers   Tick one ☑
New customers only

cancel all existing mandates given on ☐
our behalf except in relation to items
and instructions dated prior to
Barclays' receipt of this mandate,
in which case our previous mandate
will apply

Barclays is authorised to

- debit our accounts with cheques, payment orders and bills of exchange, and
- comply with instructions, including those relating to safe custody items

whether or not our accounts become overdrawn or overdrafts are increased by doing so, and provided that such items or instructions are signed on our behalf by

ANY TWO DIRECTORS

Specify the positions of the persons who are to sign (not personal names) and in what combination for example, Managing Director alone or any two Directors together

This mandate is to apply to all existing and future accounts that the Company maintains with Barclays, until varied by the Company

It is agreed that Barclays

- has the right to refuse to allow, or increase, overdrafts on our accounts, and
- may require additional documentation from ourselves for some services or facilities

We confirm that the above is an accurate statement of what was agreed at the meeting

Signature of Chairman of the meeting   Signature of Secretary of the meeting

Name of company	SINCLAIR BROOK LTD.
Company's registered number	2958141
Account number(s)	

Day Month
Date   01 . 08 . 0X

Cheques and other documents to
be signed by   ANY TWO DIRECTORS

Specify the positions of the persons who are to sign (not personal names) and in what combination for example, Managing Director alone or any two Directors together

Please complete lists of approved signatures on both parts of the form overleaf

BARCLAYS

2

Fig. 15. Example of a bank mandate.

EMPLOYING YOUR STAFF

You will recall that earlier it was seen that all the people who work for a company are employees, including the directors and the secretary. However, a new company may find it necessary to employ a member of staff if, for example, the principal director feels he must be out selling and working and needs someone by the telephone to take orders and messages and do some office work.

The most important consideration is to pick the right person for the right job. Any employee incurs some basic costs including:

- wage or salary

- employer's National Insurance contributions

- possible commission or overtime.

You must therefore make sure the company can afford to pay such a person and, if so, how much.

Deciding who you should look for

Some other considerations to take into account are:

- Is there a real job to be done?

- Could a temporary do it?

- Prepare a job description detailing the duties of the job.

- Decide where the employee is to come from. It could be a recruitment agency, advert or simply a suitable member of your family or a friend. (**Remember that you must not**

discriminate on grounds of sex, race or marital status in advertisements, interviews or job descriptions.)

- Do they need to drive?

- Do they need any training?

When taking someone on you should be careful to start the relationship properly. You must:

- tell the tax office when you take on an employee. You should get a P45 setting out the tax details of any previous employment from your new employee. If this is not produced complete a Form P46 and send it to the tax office instead.

- present the employee with a contract of employment, i.e. a written statement, setting out the terms upon which they are employed.

Understanding the contract of employment

An employment contract is an agreement between employee and employer, outlining both sides' rights and duties. It is possible to make a contract with an employee verbally but there would be no permanent record so you would be well advised to make it in writing. It should contain:

- an offer of employment from the company

- an acceptance of that employment by the employee

- the rate of pay

- anything else that makes up the terms.

If the contract is in writing it must contain:

- your company name

- the employee's name

- the job title with a brief description

- when the job began

- the place of work

- the rate of pay and when it will be paid

- the hours of work

- details of holidays, public holidays and holiday pay

- details of any pension scheme

- details of sick pay and how it is calculated

- the length of notice to be given by both you and your employee.

The employee must also be given the name of the person they should report to if they are dissatisfied with a decision or have a grievance.

As an employer you are required by law to deduct tax and National Insurance from an employee's pay and account for the collection of it to the government. You must also broadly pay equally to any employees carrying out similar work or work of equal value. And you must pay statutory sick pay or maternity pay if it is due.

You must operate the PAYE system. The tax office will send you complete details of how this works.

There are many pieces of legislation relating to the employment of staff, which are too numerous to cover in detail here. They include the discrimination laws, health and safety, minimum wage, maternity, part-time work and employees leaving for whatever reason.

The subject may seem daunting but generally speaking you can employ whoever you want to and get rid of them if they are incompetent. But you must be reasonable and give them every opportunity to explain their actions.

EQUIPPING YOUR BUSINESS

There are four ways to consider how you are going to pay for any equipment your business requires.

1. *Purchasing outright.* This may mean using the company's own money or borrowing it from a bank for the purpose. If you do this, the equipment belongs to you and will show as an **asset** on your balance sheet. However, you may be using money you can ill afford.

2. *Hire purchase.* This is a way of borrowing but the asset will not belong to your company until the end of the hire period. In all other respects it is the same as buying out right. Your asset will show on your balance sheet and the amount outstanding to the hire company will show as a liability.

3. *Leasing.* When you lease, the asset does not belong to your company. It remains the property of the leasing company. It is a useful option when money is short.

4. *Contract hire.* This is a type of leasing normally used for, say, a fleet of vehicles where the actual vehicles are not specified but the use of an agreed number is. The hire price may well include maintenance as well.

The equipment your company uses may have an impact on your customers. An efficient telephone system will give your customers confidence, but an answerphone usually means you do not have the resources to employ a receptionist. Your car will usually say something about you, but if a car is too big or expensive it may indicate rashness in your purchase beyond your means. Decent office furniture may be more efficient but more expensive.

Weigh up your means and your needs and try to select a level of standard and price which is within your capability.

ACTION POINTS AND REMINDERS

1. Make sure that the name you have chosen will be suitable when your business expands.

2. Check with Companies House that the name you want is available.

3. Have you received concessions from your bank as a new business customer?

4. It is as well to meet your bank manager as soon as possible.

5. Are you contemplating hiring any employees? If so, obtain the employer's starter pack from the tax office.

6. Will you need to buy any equipment? If so, how will you pay for it?

8

Producing Accounts

Why is it that one of the most uninteresting aspects, except to someone with an eye for figures, of any business is keeping financial and other records? Most entrepreneurs will be much more interested in chasing sales or doing a deal with a supplier, but it is a fact of life that records of all kinds are an invaluable tool to anyone in business. History tells us a lot about the future and helps answer a lot of questions. This chapter explains what record keeping is and does. It includes:

■ keeping your books

■ watching your money

■ having an audit

■ making losses

■ judging your business.

KEEPING YOUR BOOKS

Running a business in the 21st century entails keeping control of the daily deluge of paper that hits your office desk. Letters, enquiries, bills, tax demands, junk mail, invoices and mail shots are among the many bits of paper that have to be dealt with.

> The first rule in any office is **be organised**.

You must develop, as quickly as possible, a routine which suits you.

It could be that as soon as you get to the office you check the answerphone for important messages, then open the post and sort it into piles covering sales, buying and accounts. Make all the urgent telephone calls. Start the day's work.

These priorities may change as the business grows but the important thing is to have a routine which ensures you cover all aspects of the business and nothing is forgotten. Don't let your office work drift into chaos. It can be fatal.

Book-keeping

Accounting records, or book-keeping as it is more often known, are an essential part of this routine and you must set aside time to deal with your accounts data on a regular basis. Good records are needed for a number of reasons including proof of what is in your accounts and what is going on in your business. You will be required by the Inspector of Taxes and the Registrar of Companies to produce accurate accounts and the records you keep will justify the figures contained in them.

The records you keep will depend on the business but all businesses have to keep records of their cash and bank transactions. The main requirement of these records is to let you know how much cash or spending power you have at any one time.

Recording debtors and creditors

If your customers do not pay you when you sell them goods you will have to keep records of what people owe you and for how long. Similarly, you may buy your stock or goods on credit so you will need to know how much you owe and by combining the records of monies in and monies out you should begin to forecast what money you will need and when. These records will also tell you what you have spent in total, what has come in and whether you are making a profit or a loss. The more sophisticated your records the more accurate will be your results, but you should keep the records as simple as possible so that the information you get is what you want. It is no good hoping your business is successful. You must know.

If you have employees you must keep accurate records so that your duty as a tax collector for the government is properly fulfilled. This applies to VAT as well.

There may be many other records to keep. These include details of customers, suppliers and services you use. But all this takes time, a commodity which may be scarce when you start a new enterprise.

> **Keep your records simple.**

There is not sufficient space here to cover the many methods of book-keeping and you would be well advised to seek the help of an accountant to set you up with the simplest accounting procedure for your business. For some businesses there are ready-made systems and, of course, you may well be computer literate and wish to use ready-made book-keeping packages.

Summary

■ Keep your records simple.

■ Remember the records must be accurate for tax and VAT purposes.

■ Be methodical.

■ Control of your business will be difficult if your records are not adequate.

WATCHING YOUR MONEY

All companies can be considered purely in financial terms and it is in this way that effective control of what is happening is exercised. Once upon a time a businessperson might have run his or her business with very few records and some even 'on the back of a fag packet'.

Today everything is much more sophisticated and it is therefore easier to watch what is happening to your money. For example, the banks produce statements showing all your transactions with them. Not only is their system foolproof as far as the banking and cheques paid out are concerned, but also they may be entering transactions initiated or agreed by you but not generated by you directly. They may be:

■ standing orders, which are instructions to the bank to pay bills on a certain date in the month or year

■ direct debits, which means your supplier supplies his goods and takes his money out of your account with your permission

■ bank charges or interest payments which are in accordance with your agreement with your bank.

You will appreciate from this that your records may be out of date until you have verified these amounts by checking against your own books. Equally, you may have made payments to suppliers who, for some reason or another, have not paid your cheques in and so the bank has not yet reduced your balance with them.

It is therefore essential that you keep your own record of the exact amount you have in hand so that you do not breach your agreement with your bank and run into unauthorised overdraft problems.

You will also need to know how much money your customers owe for goods and services supplied to them but not yet paid for. This record is normally a sales ledger, which will show, in respect of each customer, how many invoices you have sent them, how many they have paid for and therefore how many are still outstanding.

The same system can be used for the suppliers of goods and services to you.

With these records you now know how much you have, how much you owe and how much is owed to you. If you plot this you can forecast fairly accurately what your cash position is at any time and manage your money so that you do not overspend. Bank managers will be impressed with you if you have that knowledge.

All these recording systems are designed to ensure that you do not run out of money. Remember that the VAT, if you are registered, will need to be paid at some date in the future, as will the tax if you have employees. You will also be required to pay the tax on your own income at a later date. These occurrences can all also be built into your cash planning. Finally, with good records you will be better able to plan for the future. You will be able to assess:

- how much money is available for your advertising campaign

- how you will be able to afford new equipment

- when you can have your new car.

Major projections and realistic estimates like these can only be done when the basic information is available. All good companies know their current financial situation.

HAVING AN AUDIT

It is not necessary for a small company to have an audit or appoint an auditor. The stringent rules applying to small companies have been relaxed in the last few years, and if your company: has a balance sheet total of not more than £2.8 million it may be able to take advantage of these new audit requirements. Small companies tend to have auditors who not only audit the accounts of the company but very often help the company to prepare them and assist with their book-keeping and tax matters. However, the auditor must not take part in the management of the company.

> **Note that if ten per cent or more of the members of the company demand an audit the company must have one.**

A company's first auditor is appointed by the directors. He or she holds office until the general meeting at which the first accounts are laid before the members. From then on it is up to the members to re-appoint the existing auditor or elect a new one at each subsequent meeting.

However, a private company can pass a resolution not to lay its accounts before the members in general meeting. If this is the case, the auditor has to be appointed or re-appointed at another meeting within 28 days of the accounts being sent to the members.

In addition, a private company can pass a resolution dispensing with the need to appoint an auditor every year. In that case the auditor remains in office until removed by passing another resolution.

What does the auditor do?

The auditor has a number of functions. He or she should ensure that:

■ the company has kept proper accounting records

■ the company's accounts are in agreement with them

■ the accounts comply with the requirements of the Companies Act

■ the accounts give a true and fair view of the company's affairs

■ the information given in the Directors' Report is consistent with the accounts.

When the auditor is satisfied with this, he or she gives a report to the members stating an opinion on all the abovementioned items.

Who can be an auditor?

Only certain people can be auditors. They must be members of a recognised supervisory body and must hold a current audit practising certificate. The five recognised bodies are:

- the Institute of Chartered Accountants in England and Wales

- the Institute of Chartered Accountants of Scotland

- the Institute of Chartered Accountants in Ireland

- the Chartered Association of Certified Accountants

- the Association of Authorised Public Accountants.

You must make sure the auditor of your company is registered. If you are in doubt contact his or her professional body.

It is for the directors of the company, providing it meets the criteria for opting out of an audit, to decide whether to do so. If they do not decide to opt out then the company must have an audit.

Can an auditor resign?

An auditor may resign, in which case he or she must explain the reasons to the company and be removed by not re-appointing or passing the appropriate resolution. Note that an auditor may have an entitlement to damages if the appointment is terminated by the company.

MAKING LOSSES

Nobody forms a company with a view to making a loss. But it happens.

A company can make profits or losses in three ways:

1. Through ordinary trading.

2. By capital gains.

3. On investment income.

It is not compulsory for a company to make a profit but it helps!

It is possible for a company to make a profit on accounts but make a loss for the purpose of calculating any tax payable. This may also apply the other way round. The method of calculating profits for corporation tax purposes is dealt with in Chapter 11.

Losses are basically the difference between income and expenditure where the expenditure exceeds the income for the period of the accounts. The accounts of a company must show the income and the expenditure which relate precisely to the period of the accounts.

Example

Accounts for the year 31 December 2XXX:

Income	£45,000
Expenditure	£55,000
Therefore loss is	£10,000

The losses amount to £10,000 but included in the figures for expenditure is £15,000 paid as a salary to a director. It is therefore arguable that the company made a profit of £5,000 before paying the director's salary. This would be true if it was a sole trader business, but in a company directors' salaries are a deduction from profits as directors are employees of the company. They cannot give their salary back.

It is possible for a company to make a loss on its trading activities but to make a profit on the sale of an asset, like a piece of land or equipment. Land and equipment are held for the long term and expenditure on them is not made for the current year only. However, when the asset is sold the precise profit or loss is crystallised in the current year. For both accounts and tax purposes all these losses and profits can be set off against one another.

Despite the above examples the object of being in business is to make a profit. Losses, however made, have to be paid for out of the capital in the business and will diminish the amount of money left to invest in future trading. Too many losses will starve the business of all its capital and the closure of the business will result.

Monitor your activities well and the problems caused by losses will be minimised.

JUDGING YOUR BUSINESS

The ability to know what is going on in your business cannot be emphasised enough. It enables you to plan your next moves using the experience of hindsight and gives you a clearer view of where the business is going.

This can be highlighted by producing regular, say monthly, figures. You should know your monthly sales figures and they should be broken down into products or types of sale. You can get from your books an analysis of what your expenditure is being spent on: wages, goods for resale, telephone, electricity and so on. All this information gradually builds a picture of what is happening. It shows up seasonal fluctuations. It shows what happens in the holiday month of August, when sales may be up if you sell ice cream or down if you sell overcoats. It shows what happens if the unexpected happens, like snow in August when overcoats are at a premium!

Eventually you may deem it necessary to produce a regular flow of information including a set of accounts each month, which will keep you fully informed and enable you to forecast what will happen with more accuracy. You will be able to change direction with confidence if you think fit. You will be judging your business for yourself.

Armed with this information how much easier it will be to convince others that you know what you are talking about. You can visit your bank manager with your head held high, knowing you can satisfy him or her with your answers. You are now in control of most events.

ACTION POINTS AND REMINDERS

1. Remember to keep your office organised and tidy.

2. Establish the records you will keep.

3. Records of sales and purchases should be kept if both are on credit.

4. Initially, keep only essential records and do not waste time on unnecessary information.

5. Regularly check on your cash position.

6. Will your company need an auditor?

7. If not, who will prepare your accounts?

8. Have you got sufficient information to judge your business success?

9. Check to see if your company is making a loss on any of its activities.

Raising Money

Raising money for your company needs much thought:

- What is the money for?

- How much do you need and how long do you want it for?

- Where can you get it from?

- What guarantee can you give that it will be spent wisely?

- What security have you got?

You also have to convince serious people that you really need the money and excite them into giving, investing or lending it to you. Be prepared to spend some time on this project. It may be the most important 'SALE' you ever make. So you must get it right.

This chapter covers the raising of money from a variety of sources and explains how to go about it. It contains details of:

- preparing your business plan

- dealing with your bank

- finding your sources

- borrowing money

- issuing more shares.

PREPARING YOUR BUSINESS PLAN

You cannot expect to persuade people to invest in the future of your business unless you have a clear idea of where it is going. You must have a prepared plan which you can explain to anyone interested in helping you. You often hear stories about people who start enterprises without planning them but in reality it does not happen. Whatever your idea is, it will need to be thought about and that is the first stage of your plan. You must then go into more detail. Each step must be considered, together with any alternatives, until you are sure it will achieve the objective you are seeking.

So what is a business plan?

A **business plan** can be prepared at any time. It projects your business into the future and tries to forecast what will happen. But you must have firm objectives first. It is a financial model of the future as far as your company or business is concerned.

What will it contain?

Your plan should contain the following:

- your ultimate goal

- the products or services you intend to sell

- what you will charge for the products or services

- how you will promote the business

- where you think your market is

- who your competitors are

- how you intend to manage the finances

- calculation of your break-even point, i.e. the smallest amount of sales which, in theory, produce neither a profit nor a loss

- details of premises, equipment, vehicles, etc.

- staff details

- personal details

- a cash flow forecast of the expected movements in cash over the next one or two years.

You should write up this plan as logically as you can and then re-read it to see if you can improve it. The idea is to give the potential reader a realistic summary of the current position and an optimistic view of the future without being overconfident. Overconfidence may lead to some scepticism on the part of the recipient. When you are satisfied that the plan tells the story as you see it, you must check that your cash flow figures are in accordance.

Remember

If you secure a loan on the evidence of your plan and it fails to live up to expectations you will find it hard to go back for a bit more.

The credibility of your plan will be in jeopardy.

Make sure you are totally familiar with all the aspects of the plan. You must expect to be questioned in depth about its contents.

Now you are armed with a reliable business plan you can face possible lenders of money with confidence.

DEALING WITH YOUR BANK

Your bank manager is only human. If you are a responsible business person your bank manager will look upon your request for money with sympathy. Conversely, if you upset your bank manager you will be treated accordingly. In business everyone is your friend whether you like them or not. You never know when your paths will cross again.

Anyone starting in business is naturally optimistic, but be careful when raising money not to ask for too much. You may overdo it. On the other hand if you ask for too little your business may not be viable. Try and be firm that the money your plan suggests is correct. Your bank manager may try to persuade you that you can manage on less, but if you have done your homework properly you will be able to argue for the deal you want.

Financing your set-up plans

Your plan and forecasts will indicate how much money you want and when. If you are starting your business from scratch you will need money initially for setting up. This may include expenditure in two main areas:

1. The initial expense of buying equipment, premises, marketing costs and legal and professional charges.

2. Working capital which is the money you need to pay for your goods or stock prior to selling them and receiving payment. A number of factors affect the amount of working capital a

business needs, including the amount of credit you give your customers and the amount your suppliers give you. You will need more if you hold large stocks.

Your bank manager has two main ways of funding your business: overdraft or loan.

Overdraft

Firstly, you may be granted an overdraft facility if your need for money is likely to be short term. This means you will be able to draw more money out of your account than is in there up to a certain limit. The account is run as if it were your money and a charge for the interest you have incurred is debited to your account periodically. These interest rates may vary as interest rates have a habit of doing. It will be assumed that you will repay the outstanding sum fairly quickly.

Loan

Alternatively, you may be lent money by way of a formal loan for a given period with regular repayments of both capital and interest. This may be used where larger sums are involved or where the money is required over a longer period. The rate of interest can be a fixed percentage or a variable one which will fluctuate with the movement of interest rates generally. There are a number of other variations of repayment and interest which can be negotiated.

Small Firms Loan Schemes

The government tries to ensure that small firms have the money they need to finance their businesses, both working capital and investment. There are normally guaranteed schemes which lend money at fixed rates of interest.

These schemes are forever changing according to the financial climate at any one time, but have commonly been known as the Small Firms Loan Guarantee Scheme or the Enterprise Finance Guarantee.

Details of these schemes can be found on the internet.

One other important consideration is that of **security**. A bank may well require, with certain types of loan, security which will give them the right over, for example, an asset of yours should you fail to repay your loan in accordance with the predetermined agreement. If it is the company which is doing the borrowing it may have no assets and the bank may require a personal guarantee from you that you will make the repayment should the company fail to do so. In each case this defeats your limited liability as you take on the debt personally under this agreement. You should consult your family before taking this step as they have a stake in your personal assets.

To summarise, the first impression you give may be vital. Make your plan readable but concise. Practise delivering your plan and remember you are normally dealing with fairly conservative bank managers. Don't be too outrageous yourself. If you are asked for more information get it organised quickly. Above all be yourself.

FINDING YOUR SOURCES

Banks are not the only providers of funds for new or small businesses by any means. There are many other sources. It is as well to investigate all these before you make any decisions.

Potential sources

These include:

- your own family

- your shareholders (this will be dealt with later in this chapter)

- venture capital companies

- hire purchase, leasing and finance companies

- individuals with capital they wish to invest

- local authority grants or premises

- Training and Enterprise Councils

- government loan guarantee scheme

- charities like the Prince's Youth Business Trust

- competitions, such as Livewire, for young people

- newspapers advertising competitions run by accountants, banks, etc.

Get in touch with as many of these as you can and show them you are interested. If you don't ask you don't get!

Most of these funders will require your business plan so have copies available. Their individual requirements may be different but your plan will be the basis for all of them. All the criteria for impressing your bank manager will apply to any of these funders so you must humour them. Imagine what you would be like if it was your money you were lending to someone else.

BORROWING MONEY

Borrowing money is never easy. Although you know what you want it for you will find the prospective lender sceptical, especially if you are just starting in business and you have a small company. The better your track record, the greater the chance of obtaining funds.

You will also find that lenders always like to see you put your own money into your enterprise. This gives them confidence that you are confident. Banks will often match the money you put in but are reluctant to put theirs in without some security.

Should you ask for more or less than you need?

Some people suggest that when borrowing money you should always ask for more than you need so that you can do a deal at the figure you really want when your lender beats you down. Others suggest you should be conservative. There are drawbacks in both of these approaches. The prime one is that your plan will have to be adjusted to agree with your request and this might throw your projections out. Of course, if you ask for too little and get it you are going to run into difficulties when the money runs out and you are forced to go back for more.

The sensible course is to be realistic, have confidence in your figures and be firm in your negotiations. You know more about your business proposition than your lender so use the knowledge to your advantage. You will be respected all the more for it.

In the event of failure

If you fail to convince anyone to lend you money do not despair.

1. Look at your plan again.

2. See if you can adjust it.

3. Do you need all the equipment at once?

4. Can the purchases be staggered?

5. Are there alternative premises?

6. Are your sales forecasts too optimistic?

It is important to keep improving your plan until your lender can see it will work. Go through the whole exercise again until you are sure you are on the right lines. You will be learning all the time and there is no substitute for experience. If you have a good product there must be a combination that will work.

ISSUING MORE SHARES

Mention was made earlier of raising money from your shareholders. This is always a possibility provided there are enough shareholders and that they have the resources.

Firstly, you must make sure that there is sufficient un-issued **nominal capital**. If not, steps must be taken to increase it. Unless the Articles of Association say otherwise a resolution must be passed by the company in general meeting.

Example

'It was resolved that the capital of the company be and is hereby increased from £1,000 to £10,000 by the creation of an additional 9,000 ordinary shares of £1 each.'

A printed copy of this resolution authorising the increase must be filed with the Registrar of Companies within 15 days of the passing of the resolution. Also, as this is effectively amending the original Memorandum and Articles of Association, an amended copy of those must be filed.

Once there are sufficient shares to issue care must be taken to allot any new shares fairly. Consider this simple example.

Example

Shareholders

	A	B
Shares already issued	600	400
Increase by 9,000 shares enabling £9,000 to be raised		
Allotted	3,000	6,000
New holdings	3,600	6,400

Shareholder A had 60 per cent of the original shares and therefore 60 per cent of the control. After the allotment of the new shares he only has 40 per cent and has lost control of the company to B. It is therefore important to allot these shares in the same proportions in which the holdings were originally held if a change in the control of the company is to be avoided. This may be difficult if the principal shareholder A has no money and B has. It would be better to try to negotiate a loan from B and leave the shareholdings as they are.

You must realise, therefore, that if you are willing to sell some shares to a third party you must first get the agreement of the other existing shareholders so that everyone knows the implications. You must relinquish some of the potential gains you might get as the value of the shares increases as your business grows. This, after all, is what any potential investor is looking for. And you will now have an additional person owning part of your company who may wish to exercise his or her power if events do not go as expected.

Most small companies have a clause in their Memorandum and Articles which precludes shareholders selling their shares to anyone other than existing shareholders. So the market for shares is small and the value is restricted.

It may be better to pursue other ways of raising money first.

ACTION POINTS AND REMINDERS

1. Have you got a cash problem? If so, try to identify it.

2. Have you got a future plan for your business?

3. Make sure your plan is written down.

4. Do you need some extra capital? If so, when?

5. Approach your bank first and discuss the problem with them.

6. What are your alternatives?

7. Make sure you know your business well enough financially to give a good case to a lender.

8. What is your nominal and issued capital?

9. Will you need to issue more shares?

10. Who will buy them? Remember to watch the effect on the control of your business.

10

Using the Web

No book on setting up in business in the 21st century would be complete without a chapter on the World Wide Web. Many businesses have been taken by surprise at the speed at which the internet has intruded into our lives. When you are in business you avoid the advantages of using the web at your peril.

USING THE WEB FOR INFORMATION

There is nothing worse than feeling left behind. So unless you are in the business of computers you may find the prospect of using the internet in business daunting. Admittedly, it is a steep learning curve but a relatively short one.

The internet is an international computer network with answers to all the questions you may wish to know the answer to, with the ability to send messages across the world instantly, transfer documents, obtain supplies and technical information and generally do anything with numbers, words and pictures that you can do by any other means. In business it is becoming as integral as the telephone or fax machine.

Businesses are being set up at a very fast rate currently in a frenzy of activity so you will not be alone in using it as a business tool. But don't get carried away. It is essential to decide what your business can best derive from using the web.

The setting up of a limited company referred to earlier in this book can now be done online. Company agents have websites where registration forms can be filled in and the whole process completed without you leaving your computer. Sample Memorandum and Articles can be sent to you for checking that they adequately cover your needs. Names can be checked with the Registrar of Companies to ensure their validity.

The Companies Acts and other legislation can be accessed at any time to enable you to check that you are not acting outside company law. All PAYE and National Insurance rules and regulations are available online.

Bank accounts may be opened online and access to the details of your accounts can be made using appropriate security pin numbers. Monies may be transferred from one account to another and your accounts can be managed by you without the need to contact a person at the bank to do it for you.

As time goes by and security is improved you will be able to transact almost any business which requires data transference from the comfort of your own office.

11

Troubleshooting

This chapter deals with the areas most companies and businesses have problems with. They are mainly things over which you have little control because you are dependent on others, but you must try to overcome them because they can be critical in your success. Points covered include:

■ paying your taxman

■ dealing with your creditors

■ getting your money in

■ insuring your problems

■ training for your business.

PAYING YOUR TAXMAN

How often have you heard the cries 'I hate paying tax' or 'Why do I pay so much tax?' Well, the fact remains that all businesses have to pay tax and it is only *when* it is paid that differs. The main problem most businesses suffer, however, is having the money available to pay the tax when it is due.

Income tax

To recap, tax is, in theory, paid both by the company and its employees. Remember that directors are employees so the tax on all salaries and wages is payable under the **PAYE** (**pay as you earn**) system and is collected by you. The PAYE system gives you a code number which reflects the tax allowances to which you as an employee are entitled. Tables are provided by HMRC (HM Revenue & Customs) to convert the code into tax payable or repayable if you have paid too much. The income tax year starts on 5 April and both income tax and National Insurance must be paid to HMRC once a month.

It is important to pay your tax on time.

Understanding and using PAYE Online for employers

There is a wide range of PAYE (Pay As You Earn) notices, forms and returns that can be sent and received online. Note that almost all employers are required to file their Employer Annual Return (P35 and P14s) and certain in-year PAYE forms online, including the employee starter and leaver information contained on forms P45 and P46.

Online filing is a fast, convenient and secure way of exchanging information with HMRC. It cuts down on time, administration and errors, and it means that you'll get up-to-date PAYE information, such as updated employee tax codes, much faster.

The guide sent to prospective employers tells you how to get started with PAYE Online for employers. It explains the different ways you can file online and how the free filing service on the HMRC website works. It also provides an overview of the steps involved in filing your Employer Annual Return online.

The tax office has a very foolproof method of collecting the taxes due from your company and if you are thinking about taking on employees you must be sure to have the wages and salaries system working properly. It sounds onerous but it is fairly simple and the starter pack issued by HMRC and the Department for Work and Pensions explains exactly how to do it.

Corporation tax

Once you have ensured that your taxes in respect of employees are dealt with properly you have to deal with the tax bill on the company profits, which is called **corporation tax**. This was mentioned in Chapter 5.

The first thing to say here is that the Inspector of Taxes cannot know how to charge you corporation tax if it is not known what your profit is. The Inspector does, however, have a very effective way of ensuring that you pay it. In the past a letter was sent containing the assessment of your profit, either based on evidence of your profits in the form of your accounts or estimated. Since June 1999 it has been up to you to assess your own profits.

Don't panic. You must, however, deal with this promptly. It will be as well to learn how the system works. You will probably have appointed an accountant to deal with these matters, but that does not stop the taxman writing to you because you are responsible. Let your accountant deal with the taxman and don't get into the position where both you and the accountant do some of it. You can imagine the mess that will ensue if you both do something without the other knowing. Wires get crossed and the taxman has as much difficulty sorting it out as you do.

The important thing is to get your accounts done on time as the Revenue are imposing more and more penalties for late accounts.

Keep your book-keeping up to date

Firstly your book-keeping must be kept up to date. At the end of your financial year balance your books and seek the assistance of your professional accountant to prepare figures in a proper way which the Inspector will be used to. Profits are calculated for accounting periods which will coincide with your company's financial year end. You will be required to add back charges for depreciation and substitute capital allowances instead. You must also add back any business expenses which are not allowable (e.g. entertaining) and deduct any which are. If you should make a loss you have a choice of what to do with it. You can:

- deduct the loss from other current profits

- carry back the loss and deduct it from profits of earlier accounting periods

- carry it forward to deduct from future profits

- deduct it from investment income.

How much tax do you pay?

Once your profits for the accounting period have been determined you can calculate the tax to be paid. Rates of corporation tax are fixed for each fiscal year (6 April to 5 April). Any tax due is payable nine months and one day from your year end, and your company is responsible for calculating the tax payable and for paying the tax within set time limits. There are various ways of paying, for example, direct debit, internet banking, telephone banking, BACS or credit card, but payments must be made online. If you wish to pay by cheque you will have to take your cheque and payslip to a participating post office or building society who will make the payment for you. Only when the Inspector and you agree the figures will a formal demand be made, which will be after you have sent (filed) a corporation tax return. Again, there are penalties for sending this in late. If the final demand differs from the amount you originally paid either there will be further payments to be made or there will be a refund. Both of these carry interest.

Finally, if you are trying to minimise your tax bill you must pay yourself the amount at which the tax rate on your salary is equal to or lower than the corporation tax rate on the company' s profits. After that the rate on your salary rises to higher rate tax. Don't forget that National Insurance is also payable by your company on your salary.

Details of all aspects of corporation tax can be found on the HMRC website.

The complexity of the taxation system in this country can only be touched on in a chapter like this so be guided by your professional adviser.

DEALING WITH YOUR CREDITORS

Your **creditors** are the people you owe money to at any time. You have seen how the taxman gets his money on time. Your bank may have a charge over assets of yours or a personal guarantee to force you to keep your debt to them under control. But the rest of your creditors have no such fallback position. They are in your hands as to when you pay them. They can, of course, withhold supplies from you, whether it is supplying no more goods or materials or cutting off your supply of electricity. However, the goods or services you have already consumed and not paid for are different.

You can manipulate your cash flow by planning the payment of your suppliers. If you hold up payment you increase your cash and if you pay too early you reduce your cash. Holding up payment too long may upset your supplier and make them reluctant to deal with you. Like most things it is a matter of confidence in one another.

Looking at your credit arrangements

Firstly, you should check all the credit arrangements you have with suppliers. Can the terms be extended? Or are they, like you, trying to get their money in as soon as possible? If you say you will pay a bill next week, or worse say the cheque is in the post when it isn't, you may cause your creditor to panic and either stop supplies or more drastically issue a writ.

You see there is a fine balance to cope with and you may have to seek more permanent finance to give you the elbow room to deal with your creditors properly. If you have cash problems paying your creditors late is a short term way of dealing with it, but it is a very hazardous journey if you cannot contain it.

It is possible for a creditor to investigate your status as a company through one of the credit agencies set up for this purpose. They may initially ask you to pay in cash until you have a track record. Or they may ask for one or two trade references from other suppliers of yours. If your order is very large you may get asked for a set of accounts or even a personal guarantee like the bank does. All these measures are designed to safeguard their money as much as they can.

You can help yourself by having records which keep you informed of:

- the name of your creditor

- how much you owe

- how long you have owed it

- your record of business with them.

Then establish a pattern of paying your bills, say, once a month. This creates a continuity which gives your supplier confidence and gives you the excuse that you only pay your bills at the end of the month.

Above all, be honest with yourself and make your plans accordingly.

GETTING YOUR MONEY IN

Roughly the same things apply to getting your money in as to paying your creditors. The big difference is that you will invariably be told by a supplier if you have not paid. The same cannot be said for everyone who owes you money.

The people whom you supply, your customers, are known as **debtors** and it is as well to formulate a system early on to keep track of what you are owed and keep it coming in. The following might be a plan of attack:

1. Make sure your customer knows your terms of credit.

2. Call or write, politely, as soon as they have gone past the date.

3. After seven days follow up with a fax or written letter making sure all the facts are correct.

4. After another seven days telephone to find out the problem. Are there queries on the account? Find out when they make their payments normally.

5. Keep ringing until you get a promise of payment.

> **Don't give up. Perseverance is the name of the game.**

6. If they will not speak to you try being someone else until you get the person you want. Pick your times carefully.

7. If they say the cheque is in the post, ask when it was sent, for how much and the cheque number.

8. Go and get the cheque yourself.

9. When you get the cheque bank it immediately, checking the details are correct.

10. If all this fails get on to your solicitor to start recovery proceedings. Take his or her advice about any further action.

You see the procedure to be adopted is one of continual pressure until you can establish an understanding with your customer which is acceptable to you both. The alternative is to stop supplying them.

Factoring

There is one other way of getting in your money. That is to sell your debts to raise cash. This is known as factoring. The factor takes over your records and collects your debts. He passes the money to you after having deducted his fee. This is only really a feasible method where your debts are considerable, say over £100,000.

INSURING YOUR PROBLEMS

Insurance is a necessary evil. Paying premiums to insurance companies to cover risks you hope will not happen anyway is not the most exciting job you have to do. But it is an important aspect of any company and should be taken seriously.

What risks should you cover?

Employers' liability

Covers injury to an employee. A normal amount might be up to £5 million. A certificate must be displayed at the place of work.

Motor

Normally covers all vehicles for third party damage as well as damage to your own vehicle.

Machinery

Some equipment has to be covered by law for safety reasons, but it is as well to cover all equipment and machinery. This includes computers and other office equipment.

Fire

Covers buildings and contents against fire.

Theft

Covers burglaries and theft from your premises.

Loss of money

Where you handle significant amounts of cash, cover is available.

Goods in transit

When you deliver goods either in your own vehicles or by another carrier.

Credit

Against customers failing to pay. A good record of collecting your debts is essential to get this cover.

Public liability

Covers your liability to visitors or members of the public if you cause them injury or damage their property.

Professional indemnity

If your business entails giving expert advice you will be covered against claims by your clients for damages caused by negligence.

Keyman

If your business relies heavily on one or more individuals a life assurance policy will cover the death of one of them.

Personal

Make sure you are personally insured properly to provide for your family in the event of unforeseen circumstances. This includes health and pensions.

Get yourself a good firm of insurance brokers and go through all these with them. You may find the cost of covering for all of them prohibitive but the broker will advise you on priorities in your company.

TRAINING FOR YOUR BUSINESS

You are never too old to learn, the saying goes, and that is as true of business as any other field. Training for business and knowledge of running a company can come in many ways. Some of these are:

- your friends in business

- professional advisers

- newspapers, books, television and radio, magazines

- exhibitions

- local business organisations (e.g. chamber of commerce)

■ trade associations

■ Business Links, Skills Funding Agency, Young People's Learning Agency and Local Enterprise Agencies

■ university and management training courses

■ the internet.

The list is endless. But where do you find the time? After all you might say 'I've got a business to run'. Like most other things you must set your priorities and plan to carry them out. Training should be one of them.

Anyone starting a business should go on some sort of management training course. No one is expert in everything and if you are good at your chosen trade you may not be good at book-keeping, for example. Some courses are general, giving the rudiments of a subject, and others are specialised, going into depth. Choose the one that suits you best.

Business Link

A network of Business Links has been established throughout the country designed to give information and advice to small businesses. There you will be able to get advice on courses. They will give you lists of courses available, whether they are on-the-job or classroom based, whether there are any training allowances available and the cost if any. There may be grants available or arrangements for business start-up. They will also provide facilities for business health checks, project management support and access to technology and design services. There is, therefore, together with the Skills Funding Agency, Young People's Learning Agency and Local Enterprise Agencies (Trusts in Scotland), a wide range of information available to the small business and any budding entrepreneur would do well to consult with them and find out the many ways that they are able to help.

Remember

■ Seek help and assistance, much of it is free.

■ Choose your courses carefully.

■ Join a business club if there is one.

■ Read avidly both trade and general literature.

ACTION POINTS AND REMINDERS

1. Save money regularly so that you can pay your tax when it is due.

2. If you have employees learn how the PAYE system works.

3. Get a supply of all the necessary forms from HMRC.

4. Make arrangements with your accountant to have your accounts prepared soon after your year end.

5. Check your own salary entitlement to the best tax advantage.

6. Make sure you have a suitable book-keeping system for paying the money you owe.

7. Make sure your money comes in regularly.

8. Check your insurance annually to see that all eventualities are covered.

9. Contact your local Business Link for advice.

12

Closing Down

There are many reasons for a business ceasing to trade, but in a company this has to be dealt with according to the rules. In this final chapter the various reasons are discussed in some detail and include:

- ceasing to trade

- disposing of your business

- planning your retirement

- going into voluntary liquidation

- suffering compulsory liquidation.

CEASING TO TRADE

There may be circumstances where you wish to close down your company and trade no more. Your business may be becoming unprofitable or overtaken by modern technology. You may wish to sell the shares or the assets to a competitor or just to a younger person. You may not be able to pay your debts or you may wish to retire. The fact is that whether a company is a success or a failure it is up to you what you do with it if you hold the power in the shares you own.

When the company is sold the shares pass to another shareholder who takes on all the responsibilities you once held. On the other hand, if you clear the company of its assets and retain your shareholding you may wish to end its existence. If the company cannot pay its way the law gives you no alternative but to do something with the company.

This act of extinguishing the life of a company is known as **liquidation** and the process may be either voluntary or compulsory. The difference is explained in some detail later in the chapter.

DISPOSING OF YOUR BUSINESS

It is, of course, possible to dispose of your company at any time. You may have found a suitable buyer, or another company who wants to take you over. You may wish to retire and sell your interest or you may want to pack up and go. Whatever the reason the disposal must be orderly and some statutory procedures have to be followed.

When you are selling a business you must establish whether you are selling the shares in your company or only the assets. A potential buyer may want to take your company lock, stock and barrel and either purchase the shares or use an existing company to buy the shares, in which case the company would be wholly owned by another company and become a subsidiary of it.

Selling the assets
It could well be more advantageous for a buyer to take only the assets you own and incorporate them into an existing business.

This may or may not include the **goodwill** (which can usefully be described as the ability to make a profit). You would be left with the company liabilities to pay and the money paid for the assets you sell. On the other hand, you may sell the whole business, including goodwill, for a given price and finish up with a company which contains only cash. Whichever way the sale goes you will have achieved your goal of selling and be left with the money in your company.

The next problem is to get the money out. It could be used to invest in another business run through the same company. However, if you wish to remove the money from the company inevitably the taxman is hovering around to take a share of the spoils. Tax is normally only payable if you realise the gain and take it away. You can also obtain some relief from inheritance tax if you give away business assets.

Selling the shares

There is relief from tax, at least for a while, if you:

1. sell shares in an unquoted company

2. have been a full-time working director

3. have owned more than five per cent of the shares for more than one year

4. invest the money in another unquoted company.

If, however, you just wish to dispose of your shares and walk away you will be liable to capital gains tax on the difference between the value of the shares you bought and the value when you sold them. There is an indexation allowance for inflation during the period you held the shares. This is just like selling shares on the Stock Exchange.

You will qualify for concessions if you are 50 years of age or over and retiring as there are a number of reliefs available – for example, retirement relief. If you sell a business, give it away or sell off the assets after you have closed the business (for example, a family-owned company) there will be relief if you owned shares in the business for more than one year.

The rules of taxation are somewhat complex and again you would be well advised to seek your accountant's advice before being too hasty with your disposal.

PLANNING YOUR RETIREMENT

It is never too early to plan your retirement, however far away it seems. You will spend most of your time ensuring your company will be a success. If, when you retire, you sell it you should have a handsome sum of money to invest that will provide you with an income to live on. But don't bank on it as the company may not be worth enough when the time comes.

Very often you will have all the skills while you are working but when you leave the business there is no business left. On the other hand, you may be forced to retire because of ill health.

What happens if your business is going through a hard time when you are taken ill? Or you suffer the ravages of inflation or recession? And what will happen if you just do not accumulate the amount of money you need to continue to live in the manner to which you have become accustomed?

The only way to alleviate this potential problem is to invest in a suitable **pension** arrangement. This is a specialised subject and a financial advisor dealing with pension arrangements should be consulted. This may mean taking a company pension or personal pension, but specific advice should be sought for your individual circumstances.

Types of plan

General types of personal plan are:

- *Unit linked* – where you choose how your money is invested whether property, shares, currency, government stocks or a combination of all of them. Your potential pension fluctuates with the value of the units.

- *With profits* – where the insurance company invests your money as it thinks fit. There will usually be a guaranteed pension topped up with bonuses as the value of the investments increases.

- *Without profits* – where the pension is fixed and you know when you start what it will be.

Occupational pension schemes

You can also arrange an occupational pension through your company. It has to be approved by HMRC to qualify for tax concessions and may be administered through an insurance company or by administering the investments yourself. There are advantages to having such a scheme:

- There is no limit on the contributions and this enables you to put in much larger sums when business is good.

■ The fund can be used to provide the capital for buying premises or major items of capital expenditure.

■ Up to half the fund can be loaned to the company.

This scheme is a specialised method of acquiring a pension and you will be well advised to consult your financial adviser before doing anything.

Tax reliefs

Any tax relief you receive will always be at your highest rate and, for example, if you are a 40 per cent tax payer it means that you will only pay £600 for every £1,000 of pension you invest in. It is indeed a bargain.

Remember

■ Start your plans early, picking the most suitable plan for you.

■ Take advice.

GOING INTO VOLUNTARY LIQUIDATION

A company may by resolution go into a **voluntary** winding up or liquidation. This may be done because the company is no longer required, because it is insolvent or likely to be or it may want to reform in a different way.

Members' voluntary liquidation

This winding up may be carried out by the members provided the directors are of the opinion that the company can pay all its debts within a period of 12 months. If so, the directors call an extraordinary general meeting and make a statutory declaration of solvency. Once this resolution is passed a liquidator can be appointed. Within 14 days a copy of the resolution must appear in the *London Gazette* (the official announcement of such matters) and a copy sent to the Registrar of Companies. Also the liquidator must give notice of his or her appointment to the Registrar and in the *London Gazette* within 14 days.

If the directors make a statutory declaration without reasonable justification and the company cannot meet its debts, then they can be liable to fines or imprisonment.

The liquidator then uses his or her best endeavours to realise the company's assets, pay the creditors, clarify any claims on the company and distribute the funds. Their fees and expenses take priority over all other charges.

Creditors' voluntary liquidation

This will occur when the directors of a company are unable to declare their solvency. In these circumstances the creditors have a greater say in how the company will be wound up. The directors first call an extraordinary general meeting to consider the winding up in the context of not being able to pay its creditors. Within 14 days of this meeting the directors must call a meeting of creditors and present them with a financial statement of affairs, verified by affidavit, and answer any questions put to them by the creditors. A liquidator may have been appointed at the first meeting and if so the creditors may approve the appointment or appoint another in his or her place.

The liquidator then takes control of the company and realises the assets. After his or her expenses he or she will distribute the funds available paying in the following order:

1. His/her own fees and expenses as liquidator and the costs of the liquidation.

2. The preferential creditors, which includes monies owed to employees and any rates or taxes due.

3. The secured creditors – i.e. those creditors with a charge over certain assets of the company.

4. The unsecured creditors – i.e. the rest of the people to whom the company owes money.

5. The balance, if any, to the shareholders in the proportion of their shareholdings.

The liquidator's appointment must be advertised in the *London Gazette*, as with a members' voluntary liquidation, and notified to the Registrar within seven days. The creditors may appoint a liquidation committee to monitor the work of the liquidator and, if thought fit, to fix his or her fees.

The end of the road

In both cases, on completion of the distributions, the appropriate forms, including a receipts and payments account, are submitted to the Registrar by the liquidator and the company no longer exists.

Suffering compulsory liquidation

There can be circumstances where a company is wound up by the court. These include, amongst other things, where:

- the company passes a special resolution to that effect

- the company does not commence business within a year, or suspends its business for a whole year

- the company is unable to pay its debts

- the court is of the opinion that it is just and equitable that the company should be wound up.

The procedure is started by those persons entitled to present a petition to the court. They include the company, the directors, a creditor or creditors, any shareholder or the clerk of a magistrates' court.

When the court makes the winding up order, the Official Receiver becomes the liquidator of the company. The directors are required to submit a statement of affairs and be interviewed. The Official Receiver can then decide to call a meeting and ask the creditors and shareholders if they wish to appoint another liquidator instead. If the Official Receiver does not advise them of such a meeting 25 per cent of the creditors in value may require it to be done.

The liquidator, or the Official Receiver, will then carry out the liquidation of the company and realise and distribute the assets. The Registrar of Companies must be informed that a liquidator has been appointed and advertised in the *London Gazette*.

There is, however, usually a good reason why someone petitions to wind up a company and if fraud, embezzlement or any other crime where the directors are involved is suspected the liquidator must inform the Secretary of State and within six months produce the evidence for this. Equally, the Secretary of State may have appointed inspectors to investigate a company on the grounds that it has been fraudulently mismanaged and may petition if he or she thinks fit.

Any company finding itself in this position probably deserves what it gets.

ACTION POINTS AND REMINDERS

1. Remember if you want to sell your business, you can sell the assets without selling the shares.

2. If you want to retire, is there enough value in your business for you to retire on?

3. Have you got a personal pension arrangement?

4. Does your company have an occupational pension scheme?

5. If you want to close your company down, make sure the reasons are clear.

6. If your company cannot pay its debts you must close it down. You will be forced out of business if you don't.

Glossary

Accountants. Professional experts in finance, business purchase, accounting and tax.

Allotment of shares. The allocation of shares by the directors to the first shareholders of a private company.

Annual General Meeting (AGM). The annual meeting of a company which considers the accounts, the auditor's report, any resolutions, the appointment or re-appointment of directors and auditors, the proposal of dividends and any other general business of the company.

Articles of Association. The internal regulations governing the management of a company and the relationships of its members with each other and with the company.

Asset. Any item of value owned by a company.

Authorised capital. The amount of share capital, declared in the Memorandum, which the company is authorised to issue.

Balance sheet. A statement of the worth of a company at an accounting date.

Benefits. Amounts paid to employees of a company other than in money.

Business. Any entrepreneurial enterprise carried out in return for money or value.

Business plan. A plan prepared to convince others that a company is viable.

Capital. The value of the shares in a company.

Certificate of Incorporation. A document signifying that the members of a company have become a body corporate and statutory requirements have been complied with.

Companies Acts. Parliamentary legislation referring to the conduct and administration of companies.

Company. An artificial person or corporation created by law and endowed with perpetual succession, and existing apart from its members.

Company registration agent. One who deals in the formation of companies on behalf of customers.

Company secretary. The chief administrative officer of a company who has statutory recognition under the Companies Act 1985 and who has ostensible authority to enter into contracts of an administrative nature on behalf of a company.

Creditors. Those persons and corporate bodies that a company owes money to.

Debtors. Those persons and corporate bodies that owe money to a company.

Debts. Amounts owed to a person or corporate body.

Director. There is no statutory definition of a director but a director is one who acts as agent in any transactions entered into on behalf of the company and as trustee of the company's property and money.

Directors' report. The annual report of the directors to the members of their stewardship of the company.

Dividend. Amounts of profit paid to shareholders in proportion to the shares they hold.

Domicile. The administrative area, under the Memorandum, in which a company is based.

Drawings. Amounts of cash or worth withdrawn by its owner from a business which is not a company.

Extraordinary general meeting. A special meeting for the purpose of putting extraordinary or special resolutions before the members of a company.

Finance Act. The Act of Parliament initiated by the Chancellor of the Exchequer covering financial matters and containing those parts of the Budget passed by Members of Parliament.

Firm. A collection of individuals bound in partnership for the purpose of carrying out a business.

Fringe benefits. See Benefits.

Goodwill. The added value which accrues to a business over and above the true net value of the net tangible assets by reason of its ability to earn profits in excess of normal profits expected from the risk capital and labour involved.

Issued capital. That portion of the authorised capital that has been subscribed for.

Joint shareholding. Shares owned by more than one person together as one holding.

Joint stock company. An incorporated company which could hold property and sue and be sued in its own name, but where the liability of the members remains unlimited.

Liabilities. Any money or money's worth owed to a person or corporate body now or in the future.

Limited liability. The restriction of the contribution of a shareholder to the nominal value of the shares he has purchased.

Members. Shareholders in a company.

Memorandum of Association. A registered document which defines a company's status, name and powers.

Nominal capital. See Authorised capital.

Objects clause. The clause in the Memorandum which sets out the purposes and powers of the company.

Off the shelf. A ready-made company from a company registration agent.

Paid up capital. That proportion of the issued capital that has been paid for.

Partnership. The relationship which subsists between persons carrying on a business in common with a view to profit (Partnership Act 1890).

Pay as you earn (PAYE). A scheme where employers have to deduct income tax and National Insurance from employees' wages and salaries each month and pass them to HMRC.

Pension. An insurance arrangement to provide a fund out of which the subscriber will be paid during retirement.

Profit. The excess of income over expenditure for a given period of time.

Profit and loss account. An account summarising the income and expenditure of a company and showing whether it has made a profit or a loss.

Proxy. A shareholder who is appointed by and acts and votes for another shareholder at a general meeting of a company.

Quorum. The number of people required to attend a meeting to make it valid.

Registered office. The official address of a company which has been submitted to the Registrar of Companies as such.

Registrar of Companies. The chief officer of Companies House, which is the executive agency of the Department for Business Innovation and Skills, dealing with the incorporation, regulation and dissolution of companies under the Companies Acts and the provision to the public of information about these companies.

Resolution. The means of getting agreement to a course of events by the shareholders of a company.

Security. Assets put up as collateral or guarantee against loans.

Share. The title of ownership of a stake in a company.

Share capital. See Capital.

Share certificate. The document issued to a holder of shares in a company to prove entitlement to them.

Shareholder. The owner of shares in a company.

Sole trader. A self-employed proprietor of a business.

Solicitors. Those professional experts dealing with the law.

Stock transfer form. The document which transfers shares from one member to another for value.

Surveyors. Those professional experts dealing with all matters in connection with property and land.

Turnover. The aggregate sales of a company.

Useful Reading

This book has been written as a guide to the entrepreneur who specifically feels the need to run a business through a company.

There are many books published on the various aspects of starting and running a business. These cover topics like:

Being your own boss
Business opportunities
Earning money from home
The first twelve months in business
Getting started
Home is where the office is
Preparing business plans
Small business finance.

The major banks also produce books and guides to help the budding entrepreneur.

However, it is recommended, after studying this book, that further information is obtained for specific purposes from one of the organisations listed overleaf.

SOURCES OF INFORMATION

This list gives you contact organisations that can be of help to you. The addresses and telephone numbers, where applicable, will be found on the relevant organisation's website.

ACAS

Accountants

Advertising Standards Authority

Association of Independent Businesses

Banks

British Franchise Association

BSI Standards

Business in the Community

Business Link

Confederation of British Industry (CBI)

Chambers of Commerce

Chartered Institute of Marketing

Chartered Institute of Personnel and Development

Chartered Institute of Public Relations

Companies House

Conferences

Department for Business, Innovation and Skills

Department for the Environment, Food and Rural Affairs

Department for Work and Pensions

Dun and Bradstreet

Education Colleges

Enterprise Agencies

Exhibitions

Federation of Small Businesses

Forum of Private Business

Health & Safety Executive

HM Revenue & Customs

Information Commissioner's Office

Institute of Certified Business Counsellors

Institute of Directors

Institute of Promotional Marketing

Intellectual Property Office

Job Centre Plus

Law Society

Libraries

Livewire

Local Authorities

National Insurance Contributions Office

National Market Traders' Federation

Office of Fair Trading

Open University

Prince's Youth Business Trust

Solicitors

Tourist Boards

Trade Associations

Trading Standards Institute

Wyvern Business Library

Yellow Pages

Youth Enterprise Service

Index